PUFFIN BOOKS

THE ALIENS ARE COMING

Have you heard about the greenhouse effect? Do you know about global warming? Most scientists agree that the world is getting warmer and that this will affect every single person on Earth. But no one really knows what effect global warming will have on wildlife and the countryside, except that some plants will not survive whilst others will flourish and become a nuisance.

In this book you'll be able to find out for yourself how the changes in the climate will bring about changes to the plant world. There are experiments for you to do so that you too can become a scientist and help predict the future.

You'll also be able to find out about aliens such as the exploding plant from the land of the yeti, the knotty problem from Japan, the monster in your garden lawn and the 1790 from Mount Etna!

Curious? Can't wait to start? Then put on your scientist's hat, open up the book, and begin!

Phil Gates is a lecturer in Botany at Durham University. He specializes in making science fun and writes regularly for the *Independent on Sunday* and the *Guardian* on botanical matters. This is his first book for children. He lives in Crook, County Durham, with his wife and three children.

THE ALIENS ARE COMING

Plant Life and the Greenhouse Effect

Illustrated by Julia Cassels

PHIL GATES

PUFFIN BOOKS

This book is dedicated to all the children
who will have to clear up the mess
that adults leave behind

PUFFIN BOOKS

Published by the Penguin Group
Penguin Books Ltd, 27 Wrights Lane, London W8 5TZ, England
Penguin Books USA Inc., 375 Hudson Street, New York, New York 10014, USA
Penguin Books Australia Ltd, Ringwood, Victoria, Australia
Penguin Books Canada Ltd, 10 Alcorn Avenue, Toronto, Ontario, Canada M4V 3B2
Penguin Books (NZ) Ltd, 182–190 Wairau Road, Auckland 10, New Zealand

Penguin Books Ltd, Registered Offices: Harmondsworth, Middlesex, England

First published 1992
10 9 8 7 6 5 4 3 2 1

Text copyright © Phil Gates, 1992
Illustrations copyright © Julia Cassels, 1992
All rights reserved

The moral right of the author has been asserted

Printed in England by Clays Ltd, St Ives plc
Set in $11\frac{1}{2}/13\frac{1}{2}$ pt Lasercomp Sabon

CONTENTS

HOW TO USE THIS BOOK

You may have heard about the greenhouse effect and global warming on the news programmes on television. Scientists agree that the world is getting warmer. No one really knows exactly what effect this will have on wildlife and the countryside. *You* are going to find out.

The only way to learn about what is going on is to do some scientific experiments. In this book there are experiments that will show you how plants react as the weather changes. If you carry out all of them, you should be able to predict how global warming might change our countryside.

To do the experiments you will have to collect materials and objects that you should find lying around the house, to make pieces of equipment. You will find a section at the back of the book which tells you where to get other items that you might need.

There are places in the book where you might find scientific words that you have not heard before. If you find any words that you do not understand, which are marked in **bold type**, look them up in the Scientific terms section at the back of the book. You will find a short explanation of what they mean.

In this book you will find stories about plants from distant countries. Use books in the library to find out about the countries and the people that live in them. Global warming will affect every single person on Earth. If you really want to know how climate changes will affect our planet, you need to know about every part of those changes.

1

AAARGH! ALIENS!

Look out of the window. There are **aliens** outside. You probably pass some every day on your way to school.

Out there, in the garden, in the fields, in the hedges and in the woods, there are alien plants from foreign lands.

Some have arrived by accident. Plants can move around more than you might think. Sometimes they travel as sticky or hooked **seeds** that can be carried on clothes. Some seeds are blown in the wind, others can travel around in the mud on your shoes or on car tyres.

Alien plants are often brought back from far-away places by explorers, so that we can grow them in our gardens.

A few alien plants like it here so much that they have already spread to every corner of the land. Lots more are out there, waiting for their chance to invade. When will they come? What are they waiting for? Where will they live? As scientists, it is our job to find out!

Some have been here so long and are so common that you might think they have been here for ever. **Botanists**, who are the scientists that study plants, have been watching them closely for a long time. Here are the true stories of five very successful aliens.

• The monster in your garden lawn

Beside a lake in ancient Greece there lived a monster with a hundred heads, called Hydra. If one of Hydra's heads was cut off, it quickly grew two more. In the lawn in your garden you probably have a plant which behaves in the same way.

The plant is slender speedwell and it comes from Turkey, which is not far from Greece.

Slender speedwell has a secret. Most plants grow from seeds which fall on to the soil and grow into a new plant, but in Britain this one never produces any. Instead, it grows from tiny pieces of stem.

If you cut it up, just like Hydra, each bit grows back into a new plant. Every time you mow your lawn, every little piece that is not collected in the grass-box on the lawn-mower will grow into a new plant.

Slender speedwell first arrived in Britain in the early 1800s and was grown as a garden plant. By 1920 it had escaped over the garden wall and has been rampaging through lawns ever since. In less than one hundred years it has spread throughout the whole country.

• The dangerous giant from Russia

Along the banks of rivers in southern Russia you will find a plant called giant hogweed, which sometimes grows over ten feet tall and has flower heads as large as cart-wheels.

Many years ago gardeners brought it to Britain, to plant in their flower borders. Anything that large was sure to impress the neighbours.

Soon, it escaped and found its way back to the river bank. It has been spreading ever since.

Giant hogweed is dangerous. The **sap** in its stems will make your skin come up in blisters. **IF YOU FIND SOME, NEVER TOUCH IT.** Because it is so harmful, an Act of Parliament has made it illegal for people to grow it deliberately.

The poison sap is giant hogweed's defence weapon. Very few grazing animals will feed on such a dangerous plant, so it can produce seeds in safety. It is still spreading, in spite of efforts to get rid of it.

• The exploding plant from the land of the yeti

Rivers flow from the melting snows of the Himalayan mountain range in Tibet, where legend has it that abominable snowmen, sometimes called yetis, roam amongst the peaks. The river banks are lined with pretty pink flowers. The same flowers can be found along rivers in Britain.

If a yeti was strolling along a river bank in Yorkshire and came across them, he would feel quite at home. The flowers are called Himalayan balsam. Once again, they are garden plants that have escaped into the wild.

Himalayan balsam has another name, policeman's helmet. If you turn the flower upside down you will see why. It is shaped very much like a policeman's helmet.

Once bees have visited the flowers, seed pods grow and these have a surprise in store. If you touch one as it ripens, it suddenly explodes and scatters seeds in every direction.

Often, the seeds land in the river and are carried downstream until they are washed up on a mud bank. There they spend the winter. When the warm weather arrives in spring they grow into a new plant.

• A knotty problem from Japan

When people first planted Japanese knotweed in their gardens, it seemed like a good idea. Because it grew quickly and covered up bare ground, it appeared to be just the plant that impatient gardeners needed. The trouble was, it wouldn't stop growing. Soon gardens were choked with the

plant. Its creeping underground stems spread with frightening speed, under paths and fences and out into the countryside.

Desperately, gardeners dug it up and threw it away on rubbish tips. Soon, it began to cover the rubbish tips, creeping underground and smothering other plants in a dense forest of two-metre-high stems as it invaded the surrounding undergrowth.

Be warned. *Never* plant Japanese knotweed!

• The plant arriving at platform 4 is the 1790 from Mount Etna

Every now and then Mount Etna, a volcano in Sicily, spews out smoke and flame and boiling lava. As the lava cools, it turns to a grey ash. Tiny, feathery seeds of a plant called ragwort drift in on the wind. They are amongst the first plants to grow on the ash. Their bright yellow, star-shaped flowers make a cheerful splash of colour against the black volcanic rock.

A botanist brought some ragwort back to England in 1790 and planted it in a botanic garden in Oxford. There it stayed until George Stephenson invented the first passenger railway in 1825. Soon, railways were criss-crossing Britain like a steel spider's web.

One of the most famous lines was the Great Western Railway, which passed through Oxford. There the engine-drivers would pause to rake out the ash from the railway engines' fires on to the track. If you had seen the ash, you would have noticed that it looked a lot like the ash on the slopes of Mount Etna.

One fateful day a feathery seed blew from the botanic garden towards the railway station. Perhaps it landed on the ash from a steam engine. No one knows for sure. The

ragwort, which gardeners now called Oxford ragwort, began to spring up around the station and produce more feathery seeds.

Every day in summer, speeding express trains carrying holiday-makers from Paddington station in London to the beaches of Devon and Cornwall thundered through the station. As they hurtled through, thousands of seeds were sucked up in the wind that the train created and were carried down the track behind the disappearing carriages. Sometimes a seed would drift in through an open carriage window, then drift out again a few miles down the line. Slowly but surely, Oxford ragwort was carried by trains along the whole of the Great Western Railway.

These are just a few amazing stories about five alien plants that have come to Britain. They have made our countryside more interesting, bringing a hint of exotic foreign lands to our rainy island.

If you look in an atlas, you will see that some of them are a very long way from home. A few of these aliens have become a bit of a nuisance as weeds, others have just made the countryside more colourful. Each is interesting in its own way.

What is it about them that has made them so successful? Firstly, they can all spread quickly when they get a chance to escape from gardens. Exploding fruits, feathered seeds and creeping stems have all given them a head start in the race to take over any suitable bare ground that becomes available. Once they are established, they can spread rapidly. Sometimes they spread so fast that they push out plants that are already there.

Secondly, we have given them a helping hand, by introducing them in the first place. Then we created **habitats**, or homes, like piles of ash and rubbish dumps, that suit them. By our activities, like building factories or ploughing fields, we create lots of bare, disturbed soil that plants can invade.

Thirdly, some, like the giant hogweed, can defend themselves against **predators** that might eat them. Others, like slender speedwell, can regrow if bits get eaten.

Most important of all, although they all come from foreign countries, they can live and multiply in our cool, wet climate. They feel at home here.

There are hundreds more alien plants that live in Britain. So far many of them have not been able to spread much. Often, they just live in small colonies, and some types are quite rare. But they might not be for much longer.

Our climate may be changing, because of the **greenhouse effect**. When the greenhouse effect takes hold, summers in some parts of Britain will get hotter and drier. Some of the plants that like a cool, wet summer will die out. New aliens are ready to step into the spaces that they leave behind.

When the winters become warmer and wetter, and snow and frost appear less often, some exotic plants from hotter countries will survive better and produce more seeds.

So when the climate changes there will be winners and losers. Which plants will win? It all depends on *how* the climate changes.

THE HEAT IS ON

What would you like first, the bad news or the good news?

The bad news is that snowmen may become an endangered species. The good news is that in future you may need to eat more ice-cream to keep cool in summer. Blame it on the greenhouse effect.

Everybody in Britain talks about the weather. On the rare occasions when we get a few weeks of hot, sunny weather it usually makes front page headlines in the newspapers. Recently, the weather has been in the news a great deal, because the world is getting warmer. We are all living in a greenhouse.

In about fifty years' time – perhaps even sooner – we will all notice that the weather has changed. No one is sure just how quickly it will happen or how large the change will be, but many scientists think that by the year 2050 summers will be much hotter and winters will be warmer and wetter.

According to some weather forecasters, we may never see snow in winter. Unless we go abroad for our holidays, we may never make a snowman or throw a snowball again. Summers may be so hot that palm trees will grow in London.

Sunshine, rain, wind, snow and ice are all different types of weather that combine to make the **climate** that we live in. For as long as people have talked about weather, Britain's climate has been cold and wet in winter and cool and wet in summer. Sometimes there are unusual years like 1989 and 1990, when we have really hot summers. These were both two-ice-creams-a-day sort of summers, but we don't usually get many of those.

Sometimes, winters have been especially cold. In the winter of 1979 it snowed so much that the snow drifted right over the roofs of some people's houses. In 1963, the sea froze in some harbours around the coast. Most people can remember rare hot summers or freezing winters, but Britain is usually just rather cold and wet. Everyone says so. Especially tourists from abroad who come here for their holidays.

Now the winters are becoming warmer and the summers are getting hotter. The reason for the change is because of something that scientists call the greenhouse effect, which is caused by **greenhouse gases** in the **atmosphere**. It works likes this:

The glass in a garden greenhouse lets sunlight through, which warms up the soil, flowerpots and plants inside. As they get hotter they release heat, like the radiators in the heating system of a house or a school. The glass lets sunlight through, but it traps the heat, stopping it from escaping again. So the air in the greenhouse gets warmer

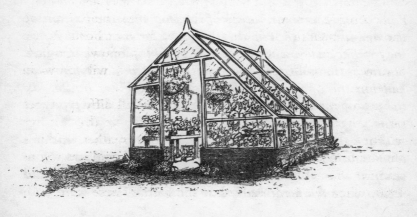

and plants grow faster than they would in the cooler garden outside.

On a clear, sunny day, the greenhouse can work so well that it can get too hot. Then the plants will die, unless you open the door or window to let the heat escape. Even on a cloudy day, it feels warm inside a greenhouse.

The greenhouse effect keeps the earth warm. Without greenhouse gases there would be nothing to stop heat escaping into outer space. The earth would cool down to about minus 18 degrees centigrade! That is colder than the freezing compartment of your refrigerator. We would enter another **ice-age** and Britain would feel like the Arctic. There would be polar bears in Birmingham and we would need to learn the skills of the Eskimos to survive.

A greenhouse experiment

You will need:
1 *A small thermometer*
2 *Some dry soil*
3 *A pair of scissors*
4 *Some sticky tape*
5 *A two-litre and one-litre clear plastic bottle, both empty*

Pour a one-centimetre layer of dry soil into the bottom of the one-litre bottle. Put the thermometer inside and screw the top back on the bottle. Now cut the top off the two-litre plastic bottle with scissors (Careful! Ask an adult for help) and put the one-litre bottle inside the two-litre bottle. Fix the top of the two-litre bottle back on with sticky tape and stand the bottles in a sunny place.

Leave them there for about half an hour, then read the temperature from the thermometer and write it down. Now separate the bottles again, remove the thermometer and measure the temperature outside the bottles.

A GREENHOUSE EXPERIMENT

YOU WILL NEED

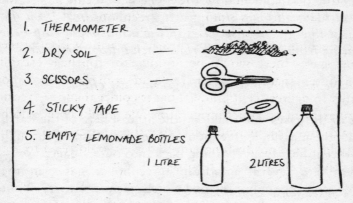

1. THERMOMETER —
2. DRY SOIL —
3. SCISSORS —
4. STICKY TAPE —
5. EMPTY LEMONADE BOTTLES

1 LITRE   2 LITRES

THE EXPERIMENT

1-LITRE LEMONADE BOTTLE
THERMOMETER
DRY SOIL

SCISSORS
2-LITRE LEMONADE BOTTLE

STICKY TAPE

LEAVE FOR ½ HOUR
IN A SUNNY PLACE

RECORD TEMPERATURE INSIDE LEMONADE BOTTLE

TEMPERATURE
1......°C

RECORD TEMPERATURE OUTSIDE BOTTLE

TEMPERATURE
1......°C
2......°C

*You will see that the temperature inside the bottles, which act like a mini-greenhouse, is higher than outside. The clear plastic lets the Sun's rays in to heat up the soil, which, in turn, heats the air above it, just as the Earth does. Meanwhile the plastic walls of the bottles and the air layer trapped between them slow down the loss of heat from the soil, just like greenhouse gases in the atmosphere stop heat **radiating** from the Earth's surface back into outer space.*

You have just demonstrated the greenhouse effect.

Some of the gases that make up the atmosphere of the Earth act like the glass in a greenhouse. They let sunshine through but prevent heat from escaping back into outer space.

There are several important greenhouse gases in the Earth's atmosphere but the one which scientists worry about most is called **carbon dioxide**. (Scientists call it CO_2, for short.) Animals breathe in **oxygen** (O_2, for short) from the air and breathe out CO_2. You release CO_2 through your nose all day long, as you breathe out.

Plants do the exact opposite. Their leaves absorb carbon dioxide and release oxygen. They can convert CO_2 into all the chemicals that they need to make them grow.

A bag of crisps starts life as CO_2, which was absorbed by a potato plant and converted into a chemical substance called **starch**. The potato that was used to make the crisps was mostly made of starch.

For as long as plants and animals have existed, the animals have produced CO_2 and plants have used it, keeping the amount of the gas in the atmosphere more or less the same. Then humans discovered fire.

When we burn coal, oil, gas, wood and most other substances we release a lot of carbon dioxide. If we cut down forests at the same time, there are fewer plants to absorb it, so more CO_2 builds up in the air. Now we have burned so much fuel, in power stations, factories and in cars, and cut down so many forests, that the amount of CO_2 in the atmosphere has risen. By the year 2040 there will be twice as much CO_2 in the air as there was in 1860.

Because of this, the Earth's greenhouse is becoming more and more efficient and the climate is getting warmer. The greenhouse effect is becoming more powerful all the time, even as you read this book.

If we did not do something to stop it, the Earth might become hotter and hotter, until all the water dried up, all the land became a desert and all the plants and animals died. Now, everyone is working to find ways to make sure that the greenhouse effect does not get out of control, allowing such a disaster to happen.

It is the Sun which keeps our planet warm. The Sun is a giant burning star, a fiery furnace of gases that creates the light and heat that strike the Earth as our planet rotates around it.

At night, when the Sun sinks below the horizon, the Earth grows cold. Overhead, in the inky blackness of the night sky, the countless, distant stars that you can see from your bedroom window are all suns, massive balls of fire that are so far away that they look tiny in comparison with our own sun.

Those distant stars also have planets like Earth rotating

around them. Somewhere out there alien life may be lurking, but it is so far away that we would have to travel at fantastic speeds for hundreds of years to reach it and find out for sure. None of us could ever live long enough to be able to make the journey and return.

But there are aliens closer to home. They are growing in your back garden now, waiting until the greenhouse effect changes the climate so that it is more to their liking. When that day comes they will be on the move. With a bit of detective work, we should be able to guess which ones will be the first to conquer your backyard.

3

THE BIG GREEN RAIN MACHINE

Imagine that you are an eagle, soaring on the rising air currents above the Amazon **rain forests** of South America. Below you stretches a dense sea of green tree-tops in the steamy jungle. Up here, high above the trees, the air ruffling your feathers is cool and clear.

You rise with the air currents that carry you towards the giant thunder-clouds billowing upwards. Suddenly, a bolt of lightning crackles across the sky, quickly followed by the roar of thunder. A raindrop splashes on your wing. And then another. And another. Soon you are forced to glide down and take shelter under the dense canopy of leaves high in the forest, as torrents of rain pour down.

Heavy raindrops patter against leaves. They collect in fat droplets that swell on the pointed leaf tips, then slip off and fall to the forest floor below. Soon small rivers run down the tree trunks. Pools of water collect on the ground.

The rain stops almost as suddenly as it began. The thunder-clouds roll away and sun breaks through. Water droplets sparkle everywhere. Wisps of steam curl up from the forest while you preen your damp feathers.

Then you launch yourself once more into the warm air rising from the forest, towards the blue sky above.

Back home in your bedroom, thousands of miles from the Amazonian jungle, you can piece together the secrets of what happened to you in that tropical storm. The air currents that carried you above the jungle were invisible, but it is easy to show how they work.

Spiral Sid the spinning snake

You will need:
1 *A sheet of paper*
2 *A pair of scissors*
3 *A piece of tracing-paper*
4 *A piece of cotton thread and a needle*

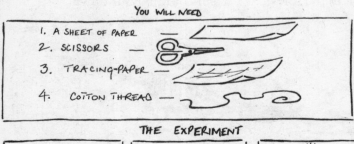

We can show how warm air rises with the help of Spiral Sid the spinning snake. Spiral Sid is an anaconda from the Amazon. Trace his picture on this page, then transfer him to a sheet of paper. Cut him out and colour him in.

With a needle, thread a piece of cotton, with a knot tied at the end, through his eye.

Now hold Spiral Sid about six inches above the bulb of a table lamp. (Do not let him touch the hot bulb!) Watch him spin round.

Spiral Sid is spinning because an invisible current of warm air is rising from the light bulb and pushing against his body.

*It was currents of warm air, rising from the jungle, that were helping to support your wings when you were gliding over it. And it was this warm air that was carrying **water vapour** up to the clouds.*

Rising air carries water vapour up into the sky. Warm air can carry more water vapour than cold air. Once the rising warm air begins to cool, the water vapour turns into water droplets and clouds form. If the tiny droplets grow too large and join together, they begin to fall back to earth as raindrops, under the pull of gravity.

You can make it rain in a plastic bottle.

Making rain

You will need:

1 *A saucer of warm water from the tap. It should be just hot enough to keep your hands in comfortably. (Ask an adult to check that it is not too hot!)*
2 *A two-litre clear plastic bottle that has been chilled in your fridge for an hour or so*
3 *An ice-cube*

Cut the top off the plastic bottle with scissors. (If you recycle the one that you used in the greenhouse experiment on page 14, this should already be done.) Put the bottle in the fridge, until it is really cold, then take it out and quickly dry it with a tea-towel.

Now turn it upside down over the saucer of warm water and put an ice-cube on the upturned end of the bottle, to keep it cold. Watch what happens.

First the plastic inside will mist up. Look carefully with a magnifying glass and you will see that the inside is covered with tiny water droplets. After a while a few of these may begin to run down the inside of the plastic, back into the saucer of water.

This is what has happened. The warm air above the water rose upwards in the bottle, carrying water vapour with it. When this warm, moist air touched the cold plastic it cooled down. Cold air cannot carry as much water vapour as warm air, so the vapour turned to droplets on the cold plastic. This process is called **condensation**.

Exactly the same thing happens when hot exhaust gases from jet engines condense to form vapour trails in the cold, blue sky high above the earth.

The same thing happens when the kettle boils. The steam is formed from tiny water droplets that condense in the cool

MAKING RAIN

YOU WILL NEED

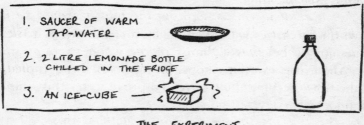

1. SAUCER OF WARM TAP-WATER —

2. 2 LITRE LEMONADE BOTTLE CHILLED IN THE FRIDGE

3. AN ICE-CUBE —

THE EXPERIMENT

SCISSORS

2 LITRE LEMONADE BOTTLE

PUT BOTTLE IN FRIDGE UNTIL REALLY CHILLED

ICE-CUBE

RAIN DROPS

air in the kitchen. If the steam condenses on the cold window pane, water droplets run down the glass.

The same thing happens when you breathe out through your mouth on a cold winter's day. Your breath looks like smoke, but it is really water vapour from your lungs condensing as tiny water droplets in the cold air.

The same thing happened when warm, moist air rose from the Amazon jungle. When it reached the cold air where you were gliding the water vapour in the air turned back to water droplets. They formed white clouds. When the thunderstorm started the tiny droplets in the clouds joined together into large, heavy drops. Like the drops on the side of your bottle or the steam condensing on your kitchen window, they fell downwards under the force of gravity, into the jungle.

So warm air carries water vapour up into the sky as it rises. In the jungle below you, most of the water vapour came from the leaves in the treetops. Water flows through plants all the time, keeping them alive. To prove it, try this simple test on a warm day.

Steaming leaves

You will need:
1 *A large polythene bag*
2 *A few large leaves from a tree like a sycamore*
Find a tree which is growing in sunshine and tie your polythene bag over the end of a branch, enclosing a few leaves.

Soon you will see that the inside of your bag has gone misty, just like the inside of your bottle in the last experiment. The water has come from the leaves. It has escaped through microscopic holes in the leaf surface, called sto-mata. They are too small to see, even with a magnifying glass.

STEAMING LEAVES

YOU WILL NEED

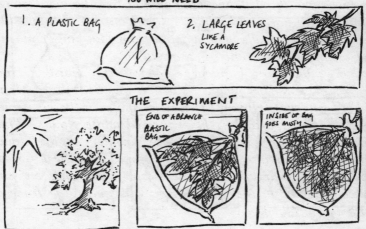

1. A PLASTIC BAG

2. LARGE LEAVES LIKE A SYCAMORE

THE EXPERIMENT

END OF A BRANCH

PLASTIC BAG

INSIDE OF BAG GOES MISTY

Leaves are connected to the roots of plants by hundreds of microscopic pipes, called **xylem tubes**, that run through the stem. They work like drain-pipes in reverse, carrying water upwards from the roots to the leaves. Once the water gets to the leaves it escapes through the stomata and is carried up to the clouds as invisible vapour.

Here's a simple trick to allow you to see xylem tubes, even though they are tiny.

Plant pipework

You will need:

1 *A white flower on a long stem – a white carnation from a flower shop will work well, or you could use any white flower that you can find in the garden. Big flowers usually work best.*

2 *Some water soluble black ink*

3 *A vase*

PLANT PIPEWORK

YOU WILL NEED

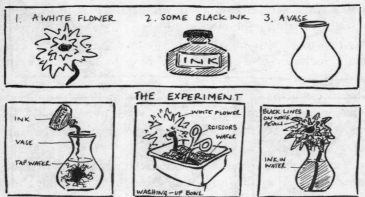

Put some water in the vase and add some black ink. Now fill a washing-up bowl with clean water and, immersing the stem of your flower in the water, cut a piece off the end of it with scissors. The reason you need to do this is that when you cut a flower off a plant its xylem tubes fill with air bubbles, so that water cannot flow along them any more. If you cut the end off under water you remove the piece of stem with the trapped bubbles and the water in the bowl will stop any more air getting in.

Now quickly put your flower in the vase of inky water and leave it overnight.

By morning you should see fine black lines all over the white petals. This is because the black, inky water has travelled up the stem xylem tubes and into the xylem tubes in the petals.

Clouds are made from tiny water droplets. Some of this water comes from the surface of the seas and rivers. Some comes from the wet surface of the soil. But a lot comes from the leaves of plants, especially trees in forests.

The Amazon forest is called a rain forest because it is a very wet place. The trees play an important part in forming the clouds. Without the clouds and the rain that falls from them, the trees and all the other plants would die. The animals, including the eagle, would have to move away, or die.

The forest helps to make the clouds that keep it alive. It is what scientists call an **ecosystem** – a living family of plants and animals that depend on one another. They all depend on the rain.

For many years now we have been cutting down or burning rain forests, turning huge areas into farmland for cattle to graze on. When the trees are all gone the clouds will not form. Rain will not fall. The grass will not grow. A desert will form.

When that happens, you, the eagle, will have vanished. If you are lucky you will find another place where the forest still grows and the clouds still form. If you are unlucky, your bones will be somewhere out there, in the lonely desert.

4

DESPERATE FOR A DRINK

All plants need water to stay alive. Some, like the cactus, can go for long periods with very little water, by closing down the tiny pores (stomata) over their surface. But if they go without water for too long, cacti die too.

To find out how long seedlings can live without a drink, try this experiment.

Wilting sunflowers

You will need:
1 *Some sunflower seeds. Buy half a pound in your local pet shop. This will provide enough seed for all your experiments.*
2 *A large flowerpot, about fifteen centimetres across*
3 *Some soil*
4 *Some cups*
5 *A clock*

*Fill the flowerpot with soil. Sow about twenty seeds by pushing them into the soil. (Useful tip: Soak the seeds overnight in water – then they will **germinate** faster.) Plant them about one centimetre below the surface. Water the soil and cover the pot with a polythene bag.*

Within about a week your seeds will have germinated and leaves will begin to appear above the soil surface. When the seedlings are about five centimetres high (2–3 weeks), carefully tip the soil out of the pot and remove the seedlings. (Their stems snap easily, so be careful not to break them!) Stand them with their roots in a cup of water.

WILTING SUNFLOWERS

YOU WILL NEED

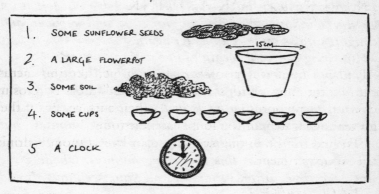

1. SOME SUNFLOWER SEEDS
2. A LARGE FLOWERPOT — 15 CM
3. SOME SOIL
4. SOME CUPS
5. A CLOCK

THE EXPERIMENT

SOIL
FLOWERPOT

WATERING-CAN
SOIL
SUNFLOWER SEEDS
FLOWERPOT

POLYTHENE BAG

1 WEEK
GERMINATED SUNFLOWER SEEDS

2-3 WEEKS

WINDOW-LEDGE

5 MINUTES
5 MINS

10 MINUTES
10 MINS

EVERY 5 MINUTES
5 10 15 20

*Now take one out and leave it on a sunny window-ledge for about ten minutes. When you pick it up you will find that it has gone floppy. It has **wilted**.*

Now put it back in the water. If you have not left it on the dry window-ledge for too long, it will recover and straighten up as it takes up water again.

How long can your seedlings live without water?

Find out by taking six seedlings from your cup of water and placing them all on the sunny window-ledge. After five minutes, put a seedling back in the water in a cup. Label this cup 'five minutes'. After another five minutes, put another one back in another cup of water. Label this one 'ten minutes'. Repeat this every five minutes, labelling the cups each time. After 30 minutes all your seedlings should be back in the water. But have they all recovered from wilting? Which was the first one to fail to recover?

Plants are made up of millions of tiny **cells**, like microscopic building bricks. Each cell is a miniature balloon, full of water. Usually they are too small to see, even with a magnifying glass. To get an idea of what they look like, try this.

Carefully peel an orange and separate it into segments. Each segment is covered with a thin skin but if you peel this off gently, using your finger-nails, you will be able to see that inside there are lots of long, giant cells. These are juice sacks, full of sweet orange juice, and if you are very careful you can separate them. Each one is a swollen bag full of sweet water. Each juice sack is really made up of several cells, but they look and behave like one giant cell.

Cells are wonderful things and come in all shapes and sizes. Some look like stars, others have walls that are almost as hard as stone. Some are full of coloured dyes and crystals. Others grow as hairs all over the outside of plants.

The sting of a stinging nettle is made from a few needle-sharp cells that inject acid into your skin when you touch them.

Now, all good scientists need some basic equipment and what you need if you are going to investigate these miniature building blocks that make up a plant, is a hand lens, that magnifies about ten times.

Better still, ask for a pocket **microscope** for a present. These are not very expensive and magnify about thirty times, which will allow you to see cells clearly. They usually have a built-in light too. If you look in the section called Suppliers at the back of this book, you will find the names of shops where you can buy these.

Best of all, you could ask for a proper microscope, that magnifies at least one hundred times. These are a bit more

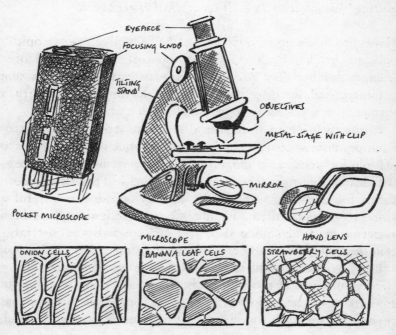

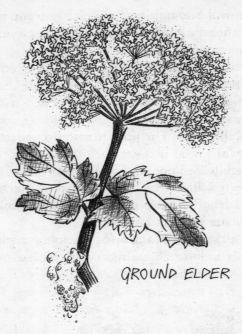

GROUND ELDER

expensive but they will allow you to see the most amazing things, like the tiny creatures that live in ponds. With a microscope you can get eye to eye with a greenfly!

But even if you have just a hand lens or a pocket microscope, you will still be able to see a lot. One good place to look for cells is in the middle of the stem of elder trees. Elder is a common hedgerow plant, so use the drawing on this page to help you identify it. Ask an adult to cut off a piece of woody stem and split it down the middle. The stem is full of dead cells called **pith cells,** which are just large enough to see clearly with a magnifying glass. They look like tiny, frothy soap-bubbles in the middle of the stem.

Another good place to find cells is inside onions. Ask an adult to cut an onion in half, from top to bottom, so that you can separate the layers. On the inside surface of each layer you will find a thin skin which you can peel off. If you look at this through a powerful magnifying glass or a pocket microscope you will see that it is made up of thousands of tiny, brick-shaped cells. The skin itself is just one cell thick.

Whole plants are made up of living, swollen cells like this. When a plant wilts, the juice inside the cells is lost and the plant collapses. The juice turns into water vapour and is carried away in the air.

If the cells become wet again they take up water and swell, like a balloon being blown up. When your seedlings recovered from wilting, it was because the cells were filling up with water again.

If you leave your orange juice sacks on a plate in a warm room, they will go floppy and wilt just like your seedlings. This is because the sacks have lost water. If you put them into a glass of water they will swell up again. Try it.

How much water do plants need? One way to find out is to make a special piece of scientific equipment, called a **potometer**.

Measuring a plant's thirst

You will need:
1 *Some bendy plastic drinking straws. You can buy straws like this from shops that sell things for birthday parties or you can recycle the ones that you find on small cartons of drink in supermarkets.*
2 *Some of your sunflower seedlings*
3 *Some Vaseline*
4 *A bowl of water*
5 *Some sticky tape*
Take a fresh sunflower seedling and hold it under water. Trim off the ends of the straggly roots close to the base of the swollen stem.

MEASURING A PLANT'S THIRST

YOU WILL NEED

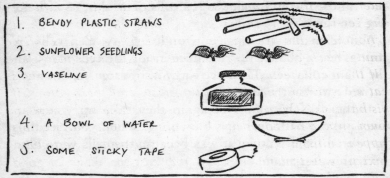

1. BENDY PLASTIC STRAWS

2. SUNFLOWER SEEDLINGS

3. VASELINE

4. A BOWL OF WATER

5. SOME STICKY TAPE

THE EXPERIMENT

Take the drinking straw and hold it under water, so that it fills up with water completely. While the straw is still under water, push the trimmed end of the sunflower seedling into one end of the straw. You might need to try out a few sunflower seedlings until you find one that fits. Make sure that you do not trap any air bubbles inside the straw, under the sunflower stem.

Now get some Vaseline and smear it around the joint between the end of the straw and the seedling, so that it makes a watertight seal. Do this while the seedling and straw are still under water. Use plenty of Vaseline.

Now remove your seedling in its home-made potometer from the water and make a right-angle bend in the straw. Blot the leaves dry gently and dry the outside of the potometer. Tape the potometer to the edge of a table, so that the long section with the open end is horizontal and the short section with the seedling is upright. Leave it for a few minutes to check that your Vaseline seal is watertight.

If the water begins to leak out of the potometer it means that air is leaking in between the straw and the seedling. If this happens, start again, using more Vaseline and forcing it down around the edges of the seedling. (Don't worry if this happens; things often go wrong in scientific experiments. Next time just make sure that the Vaseline makes a good seal.)

As the seedling uses up the water you will see the water travel back along the horizontal arm of your potometer. Measure how many millimetres of water it uses per day.

Make some more potometers and see what happens to a seedling's thirst if you stand it on a warm window-ledge or in a draught. When you do this, stand your seedling potometers in a cool, shady place first, so that the seedlings can get used to their new surroundings. Then transfer the potometers to a sunny or draughty place. Plants do not like sudden shocks.

Try another experiment. This time, cover the leaves of the seedling with a very thin layer of Vaseline, so that you block up all the tiny holes in the surface. What happens to its thirst then?

*Remember to write down the results of all your scientific experiments. You could draw out your results in a **bar chart**, like the one on the next page.*

When soil dries out, a plant's water supply is cut off. There is no water left for its roots to absorb. If it keeps on losing

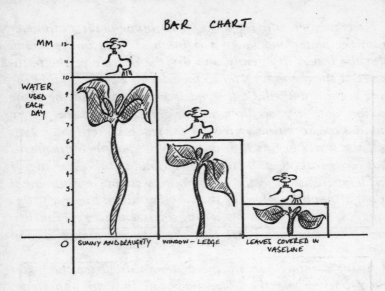

water through the microscopic holes in its leaves, its cells collapse and it wilts. Only more rain can save it.

When **global warming** takes place summers will get hotter, especially in the south of England. The soil will dry out more often. Some plants will wilt if their roots dry out. But not all plant roots are the same.

Tapping the water supply

Dig up a dandelion. This will be hard work. Dandelions have very long roots, called **tap-roots**, because they are like taps, drawing up water supplies from deep below the surface of the ground.

Now take one of your sunflower seeds and have a look at the roots. These are fibrous roots, which are very good at absorbing rain which falls on the surface of the soil. But they cannot reach the water deep down. What will happen in a long, hot, dry summer? Try this simple experiment.

TAPPING THE WATER SUPPLY

YOU WILL NEED

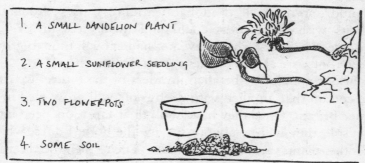

1. A SMALL DANDELION PLANT

2. A SMALL SUNFLOWER SEEDLING

3. TWO FLOWERPOTS

4. SOME SOIL

THE EXPERIMENT

You will need:
1 *A small dandelion plant. Dig it up carefully. Try not to break the tap-root.*
2 *A small sunflower seedling*
3 *Two flowerpots, about 25cm. deep*
4 *Some soil*
Plant the dandelion and the sunflower seedling in separate pots of soil. Keep them well watered for a few days, until they have got used to their new surroundings. Then stop watering them altogether. Keep them in a greenhouse or on the window-ledge, where they will get plenty of light and warmth but no rain. Check every day to see which one wilts first.

You probably guessed that the deep-rooted dandelion would survive longest. You were right. Plants like dandelions, with root systems that can reach water deep below the surface, should survive well if global warming causes droughts. Plants with short roots could find themselves in serious trouble. Seedlings, which have not had enough time to grow deep roots, are also in danger during dry weather.

In our search for the alien invaders of the future, we can be certain that an alien with deep roots will grow well in a drier Britain. Once they have sunk their tap-roots deep into the soil, they will be able to survive the hottest days, while all the plants around them wilt. Then, their seeds will germinate on the bare soil that the dying plants leave behind.

One alien which might use this trick to invade is the oriental poppy. This comes from countries in southern Europe, around the shores of the Mediterranean. Oriental poppies are like giant versions of our own corn poppies. Even their flower buds are as big as chickens' eggs and they

have long, fleshy roots that can grow about a metre down into the soil. Even if you chop an oriental poppy off at ground level its roots sprout new leaves. If you chop the roots up, the pieces will grow into new plants. And the flowers produce thousands of tiny seeds which are easily carried around on muddy feet. They have already escaped from gardens in a few places, and my guess is that, when the climate changes, their flowers will begin to spread across the landscape, like great scarlet blobs.

But not all plants will use deep roots to survive drought. For some, survival will mean a race against time.

—————————————

5

SPRINTERS AND
MARATHON RUNNERS

It's hot. Very hot. In the middle of the night your camel ran off and left you stranded in the middle of the desert.

The good news is that you still have a map. This shows that you are only ten miles from the nearest town and an unlimited supply of water. But there is an **oasis**, with a well, marked on the map. This is only two miles back up the track, in the direction from which you have just come.

The bad news is that your water bottle is almost empty. Worse still, the sun will come up soon and the temperature will soon soar to levels which will quickly leave you dying of thirst.

What would you do? Would you go back to the well, to fill your bottle, then set off for town in safety? Or would

you take a chance and race to reach the town before
sunrise?

When temperatures rise and soil dries out, plants are faced
with the same sort of problem. Some, like dandelions and
oriental poppies, draw water from the well with their deep
roots to keep themselves going. They are like long-distance
marathon runners, pacing themselves so that they can reach
the end of the race. Most plants which use this strategy are
biennials or **perennials**.

Biennials have seeds which germinate in spring and send
down a good root system. Then they sit in the soil over the
winter, with just a few leaves showing on the surface. In the
next year they use deep water supplies to produce flowers.
These produce seeds which are carried away and grow
somewhere else. The parent plant then dies. The giant
hogweed from Russia, which we met in chapter one, is a
biennial.

Perennials use the same strategy, but the parent plants
keep on growing year after year, until they eventually die of
old age. Some perennials can live for thousands of years.
There are bristlecone pine trees in the mountains of Califor-
nia in the United States which are almost 5000 years old.
Some people believe that these trees are the oldest living
things on Earth. Their seeds germinated before the Egyp-
tians built their great pyramids. These trees were already
3000 years old when Jesus Christ walked on earth.

Other plants race through life at a much faster pace.
Annuals often use small amounts of water that are available,
to flower and set seed as quickly as possible, before a
drought kills them. They are the Olympic sprinters of the
plant world.

The best place to look for plant sprinters is in habitats
that regularly dry out, like dry, sandy soils and waste places.

Many annuals are **weeds,** which means that they are plants which can be a nuisance if they grow in the wrong place, like gardens and farmers' fields. They often take the opportunity to colonize bare ground before biennials and perennials move in – and they are very adaptable plants.

Groundsel – a weed for all seasons

You will need:
1 *Three flowerpots: one small, one medium and one large*
2 *Some soil*
3 *Some sand*
Find a groundsel plant. This is a weed that you can find in every month of the year in most gardens and around the edges of school playing-fields. The drawing on this page will help you to identify it. Look for a plant that has seeds on it. These are like little plumes of grey hairs with small brown seeds hanging underneath. Collect some.

GROUNDSEL

Sow the seeds in the medium-sized flowerpot filled with soil. Push the seeds into the surface of the soil – do not cover them with a deep layer. They will germinate quickly. Once they begin to grow take two seedlings and transfer them into the small flowerpot filled with sand. Take two more seedlings and transfer them into the large flowerpot filled with soil.

Give the seedlings in sand just enough *water to stop them wilting and keep them in a warm, dry place.*

Give the seedlings in the large pot of soil plenty of water. Once they begin to grow well you can give them some house-plant food as well, but don't give any to the plants in the sand.

Now you need to make some scientific measurements. First, measure the height of the plants in centimetres every three days. Your measurements might look like this:

Seedlings in sand

Day	Height of seedling 1 (cm.)	Height of seedling 2 (cm.)	Average height (cm.)
3	1	0	0.5
6	3	1	2
9	7	5	6
12	11	8	9.5
15	15	11	13
18	18	14	16
21	20	16	18

Seedlings in soil

Day	Height of seedling 1 (cm.)	Height of seedling 2 (cm.)	Average height (cm.)
3	1	1	1
6	4	6	5
9	7	9	8
12	11	13	12
15	16	19	17.5
18	20	26	23
21	25	30	27.5

GROUNDSEL — A WEED FOR ALL SEASONS

YOU WILL NEED

1. 3 FLOWERPOTS   2. SOME SOIL   3. SOME SAND

SMALL MEDIUM LARGE

THE EXPERIMENT

GROUNDSEL SEEDS
SOIL
MEDIUM FLOWERPOT

SAND
SOIL
SMALL FLOWERPOT
LARGE FLOWERPOT

FOOD

You can see that each seedling in the sand or in the soil grew a little bit differently from its neighbour in the same pot. Perhaps one got a bit more water than the one next to it.

Scientific experiments always give slightly different results when you repeat them or use different individual living plants or animals. So scientists do not make conclusions based on one single measurement. They make several and then do a sum to work out the **average**. So that's what we'll do in this experiment.

To work out the average you add up the measurements for both the plants in each experiment, then divide that by the number of plants.

So, in the example printed on page 43, work out the average height of the plants growing in sand after 21 days by adding 20 and 16 and dividing by two. So the average height after 21 days in the sand is 18 centimetres.

You can see from your figures that the plants grown in soil with plenty of water and food grew much larger than the ones in water-starved sand.

When plants are growing over a period of time, one good way to see what is happening with your measurements is to draw a **graph**. This is a kind of picture which shows you how things change as time goes by. Scientists draw graphs all the time. This is what one looked like for my experiment. Why not draw a graph using your results.

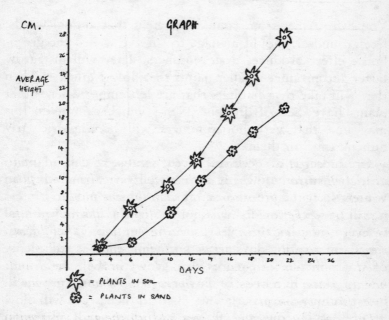

While your plants are growing you should keep a close eye on them to see which ones flower first. Write down how many days it takes before each plant flowers. Do not forget to work out the average for each experiment.

You will find that the groundsel plants in sand flowered much more quickly. This is how annuals behave when a *drought sets in. They grow as fast as they can and flower quickly, to make sure that they produce seeds before they die.*

When the plants have been growing for about a month you should count the total number of flowers on each plant and work out the average for each experiment. This time you should find that the ones in the soil, which were well watered and which grew much larger, produced a lot more flowers than the plants that grew in the drier sand.

You can predict from your experiment that annual weeds, like groundsel, should manage to survive well if the greenhouse effect produces drier summers. They will just grow faster and produce smaller plants that flower quicker. Then they will take over habitats that are left empty where other plants have died of drought. Plants which cannot do this may find that very hot summers will be a particularly difficult time for them.

Groundsel is a successful weed because it can adapt to changing surroundings. It grows well on warmer days in winter, so if the greenhouse effect produces milder winters it will benefit. Provided it is not too cold it can flower well in every month of the year, even in January. Then, when the warmer spring days arrive and while there is still plenty of water in the soil, plants that grow through the winter will produce hundreds of flowers, like the ones grown in moist soil in your experiment. Then all their seeds will blow around and grow and flower again as small plants in summer.

So it seems that groundsel will be a winner, whatever the weather.

There may also be some aliens that will do well, for the same reason. There are quite a lot of annual garden plants that have been introduced from other countries which survive

our mild winters and flower very well in the following year, even if there is a long drought.

One is an annual plant from America, called Fried Egg Plant. This has large white flowers with a yellow centre, so they look just like a fried egg.

You will find it listed in some seed catalogues under its scientific, tongue-twister of a name, *Limnanthes douglasii*. It is named after a famous Scottish collector of American plants, called David Douglas, who trekked all over North America in the early days of the Wild West, searching for interesting plants to grow in gardens. He had many narrow escapes in his travels, but his luck finally ran out when he was searching for plants in the Hawaiian Islands in the Pacific. He fell into a pit that a wild bull had already fallen into, and it killed him.

The explorers who brought these alien garden plants back to Britain often survived terrible hardships and exciting adventures in order to supply valuable alien plants for keen gardeners.

Pot marigolds, which come from Mediterranean countries, also survive mild winters and will even flower at

Christmas if there is not too much frost. Cornflowers and corncockles from the Mediterranean, larkspurs, Californian poppies, feverfew and love-in-a-mist are all annual garden flowers that will benefit from warmer winters and sprint into flower in spring. It might be a good idea if you grew some of these in your garden, to see for yourself how they perform in hot summers and warm winters. You will find them all in packets at your local garden centre. Plant them and keep a close eye on them. If the climate warms up, they are not to be trusted to stay in gardens!

6

MELTING ICE-CREAM AND TONGUE-TWISTERS

Before we go any further, this might be a good time to remind yourself about what happens when ice gets warm.

For this experiment you will need an ice-cream. Something like a large vanilla cone would be perfect. If you have trouble persuading an awkward adult to buy you one, tell them that it is a vital part of your education. If they don't let you have it, tell them your scientific career will be ruined!

Hold the cone in your hand for a minute or two and watch it closely. Notice how it turns to liquid and runs down your arm as it warms up. OK, that will do. Eat the rest of your experimental equipment.

One of the effects of global

warming will be that ice which has been frozen for thousands of years will begin to melt, just like your ice-cream. About half of all the fresh water on earth is frozen into ice. But things are changing. The Arctic ice-sheet has become thinner already, and some scientists believe that global warming is to blame.

Past ice-ages have left large sheets of ice, called **glaciers**, which fill mountain valleys in colder parts of the Earth. If the world warms up they will melt.

Most of the Arctic, in the north, is made of frozen sea. Some large areas of land, like Greenland, are covered in a thick ice-sheet, but even larger areas are made up of frozen pack-ice floating on the Arctic Ocean. If you dug down far enough through the ice at the North Pole, you would eventually get to the sea underneath.

The Antarctic continent, in the south, is a vast mass of land covered with a thick layer of ice, surrounded by sheets of ice formed by the sea freezing around its edge. Dig down through the South Pole and you would eventually reach hard rock.

The water from melting glaciers will flow downhill into rivers, which empty into the sea. As more water flows into the sea, the sea-level will rise. All over the world, water will creep a little bit further up the beach. Large areas of land will be flooded.

Some tropical islands which are only a few metres above sea-level might even disappear. The Maldive Islands in the Indian Ocean are only one metre above sea-level, so if sea-levels rise they will disappear. Most of Bangladesh will disappear under water. So will the island of Tuvalu. The canals in Venice will overflow and destroy the city. Check in an atlas to be sure you know where these places are. When global warming gets into its stride, you will be hearing a lot more about them.

Nearer to home, a sea-level rise of just one metre will mean that people living in Grimsby and parts of Kent, Suffolk and Norfolk will find that their homes are under water. The shape of Britain's coastline, and that of most other countries in the world, will slowly change.

There is another reason why sea-levels will rise when the global climate gets warmer. Like most materials, water expands when it gets hotter. You could try this experiment to prove that this is true.

A water thermometer

You will need:
1 *A plastic drinking straw, the thinner, the better. (An empty ink refill from a ball-point pen is good for this experiment.)*
2 *An empty glass sauce bottle*
3 *Some Plasticine*
Fill the bottle with water from the cold tap, then insert the drinking straw in the neck of the bottle and seal the neck

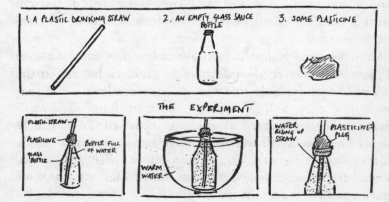

A WATER THERMOMETER

YOU WILL NEED

1. A PLASTIC DRINKING STRAW   2. AN EMPTY GLASS SAUCE BOTTLE   3. SOME PLASTICINE

THE EXPERIMENT

PLASTIC STRAW
PLASTICINE
GLASS BOTTLE
BOTTLE FULL OF WATER

WARM WATER

WATER RISING UP STRAW
PLASTICINE PLUG

with Plasticine. Now place the bottle in a bowl of water which is warm but not hot. (Ask an adult to check that it is at the right temperature.) Watch the straw. You will see the water creep up the tube as the water inside the bottle expands.

So as glaciers melt and sea-water expands, land will be flooded. Low-lying river deltas and marshes will be submerged and cities like London will be in severe danger of flooding.

When scientists need to predict the effects of change, they often make a model. Try making one for yourself, of imaginary Welly Island.

Welly Island in peril

You will need:
1 Some Plasticine or similar modelling clay
2 A shallow tray
Make Welly Island out of Plasticine. Use the drawing of the island printed here to form the hills and valleys and the outline. You can add houses, trees and people made from Plasticine if you like.

Now place the island in the centre of a shallow dish and add about 5mm. water. Then slowly add more water and watch how its shape changes. First the coastal plain and then the river valleys flood. The town of Welly-on-Sea soon disappears under the ocean and only the inhabitants of Upper Welly-on-the-Wolds will be safe, marooned on an island that is slowly shrinking.

Sea-level changes have often happened before, in the far past. The levels of the oceans have been rising and falling for millions of years. Until about 4000BC Britain was still joined to France by a land-bridge. In those days you could have walked from Dover to Calais, if those towns had

WELLY ISLAND IN PERIL

YOU WILL NEED

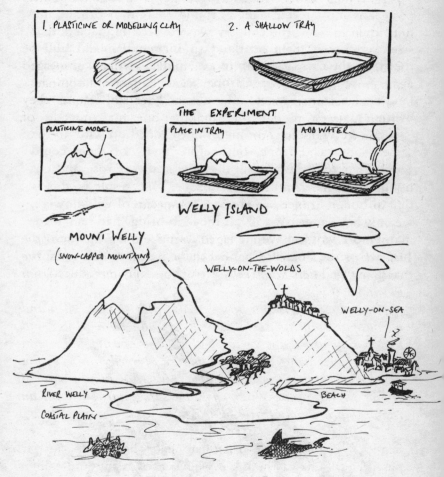

1. PLASTICINE OR MODELLING CLAY   2. A SHALLOW TRAY

THE EXPERIMENT

PLASTICINE MODEL   PLACE IN TRAY   ADD WATER

WELLY ISLAND

MOUNT WELLY
(SNOW-CAPPED MOUNTAIN)

WELLY-ON-THE-WOLDS

WELLY-ON-SEA

RIVER WELLY

COASTAL PLAIN

BEACH

USE THIS DIAGRAM OF WELLY ISLAND AS A GUIDE

existed. We would not have needed a Channel Tunnel. Our island is still very young.

What has all this got to do with alien plants? Well, several things really. There have been several ice-ages in the past. The most recent ended around 7000BC in Britain and until then most of the country was covered in glaciers that stretched down from Scotland to Birmingham. At about that time the climate began to get milder, just as it is doing again now. Plants from Europe began to move across the land-bridge from France, taking over bare soil left by the melting glaciers.

If this had gone on, we might have ended up with all the same plants as Europe, but before many of them could scramble across the land-bridge, the sea-level rose and cut us off from the continent of Europe. One result of this is that although France has about 6000 species of wild flowers, we only have a measly 1500. If the land-bridge had remained, many more would have managed to make their way across. Just across the English Channel there are many alien plants that grow well here when they are deliberately introduced.

The world has been warming up and cooling down throughout the history of life on Earth. During periods of cooling, when new ice-sheets have formed, thousands of plants and animals have been killed or driven away by freezing conditions. This has happened in Britain, in some spectacular ways.

A good example of a plant that was killed in Britain by an ice-age is a shrub called *Rhododendron ponticum*, which now grows wild in Turkey.

Tongue-twisters

Before we go any further, a few words about these long, tongue-twisting names for plants. Most plants have common names, like bluebells and harebells, for example. These are useful for talking about them amongst ourselves. You know what I mean by the word daisy, but the trouble is that not everyone speaks the same language. So a French scientist will not know what you mean when you talk about a bluebell, whose common name in French is 'jacinthe des bois'. And the French call daisies 'paquerettes'.

But he will know exactly what you mean if you call a bluebell by its long Latin name, which is *Hyacinthoides non-scripta*, or a daisy by its scientific name, which is *Bellis perennis*. These names are hard to say until you get used to them, but every scientist in the world knows plants by their Latin scientific names. Russian, Chinese, Japanese and African scientists all know plants by the same Latin names.

In fact, different meanings for common names is a problem even closer to home. If you talk to people from Scotland about bluebells, they will think you mean harebells, which are called bluebells in Scotland. What English people call bluebells become much less common as you travel north of the border. Wild hyacinth is the name that Scottish people give to English bluebells. Confusing, isn't it? It is easy to see why scientists stick to Latin names, even if they do take a long time to learn and are difficult to say.

Anyway, back to *Rhododendron ponticum*, which does not have a common name in English anyway. This is a wonderful, colourful bush with large clusters of pink flowers and deep green, glossy leaves. Scientists know that it grew here several thousand years ago, because they have found its **pollen** buried in deep layers of **peat**, in bogs. The way they discovered this fact is worth knowing, because it is a clever piece of detective work.

Pollen is the powdery substance made by flowers, which is carried to the female part of the flower, or **stigma**, by wind or insects. If you poke your finger into the centre of a flower like a lily or a daffodil, it will be coated with pollen. When pollen reaches the stigma it grows and fertilizes female eggs, called **ovules**, which are hidden in the flower. The eggs then grow into seeds.

Pollen is produced in very large amounts and often blows around in the wind. Some people are **allergic** to it and when they breathe it in they suffer from **hay fever**.

One of the amazing things about pollen is that although a single, living pollen grain is tiny (you would need a microscope to see it), it has a coat which is made of one of the toughest natural substances on Earth. The coat material is called **sporopollenin** and it lasts for tens of thousands of years, even when it is buried underground.

The second important fact about pollen is that it has a 'fingerprint'. The pollen coat has a beautiful pattern, so you can use this to recognize which type of plant it came from, just like you can use a fingerprint to identify a criminal. So if you dig up pollen grains that have been buried, you can tell which plants produced them.

This is what scientists did with the pollen of *Rhododendron ponticum*. They pushed long tubes down into peat bogs and pulled out cores of peat. Peat is made from layer upon layer of crushed, dead plants. As plants die in a bog, new plants grow on top of them and squash those underneath. So as you dig down through a peat bog, it is like taking a trip back through time.

You can tell how far back in time you have gone by using a scientific process called **radio-carbon dating**. **Carbon** can be found in all parts of plants and occurs in two different types. One type is **radioactive** but it gradually changes into a type which is not radioactive.

So pieces of dead plants, like pollen grains, have a radioactive clock ticking away inside them, as radioactive carbon slowly turns into the non-radioactive type.

By measuring the amount of radioactive carbon which is left in buried plant material, scientists can tell how long the clock has been ticking. So they can measure the age of layers of dead plants in a peat bog and work out when the pollen was formed.

Using this technique, the scientists found pollen of *Rhododendron ponticum* in peat that was formed before the last ice-age. So the plants must have been killed by the ice-sheets.

Today this plant grows wild in Turkey and has invaded some places in southern Europe. It has come back to Britain as an alien. It did not manage to return here until 1765, long after the waves closed over the land-bridge in 4000BC. Travellers brought it back to England, to grow in gardens.

To begin with it stayed within the boundaries of gardens. You can still see hundreds of plants in the grounds of stately homes. But then it began to escape and go on the rampage. It likes acid, peaty soils in areas where there is high rainfall. It has spread over thousands of acres of countryside, pushing out native plants. Large areas of the Snowdonia National Park, in North Wales, are covered in it.

It is what botanists would call a good competitor, thriving where other plants struggle to make a living and casting enough shade to smother them. It is on the march all over the country, but particularly in Wales, where landowners are fighting a desperate battle to stamp it out. When it was here before the last ice-age, sabre-toothed tigers and woolly rhinoceroses might have hidden in its dense shade. Today, it usually hides nothing more dangerous than rabbits. Sabre-toothed tigers and woolly rhinoceroses became **extinct** here long ago.

Imagine what would have happened if the last ice-age had never happened. The countryside would have looked very different and exotic plants like *Rhododendron ponticum* would be common. It would still have been a troublesome weed, but it would not have been an alien. It might have been an even worse weed than it is now. Perhaps there might still be sabre-toothed tigers lurking in it.

So ice-ages destroyed many plants that once grew here. And when the ice disappeared, Britain was cut off as an island before the original plants could return. This means that there are hundreds of plants that may have grown here in the past that could grow here again, if they were given the chance. There are lots of habitats that could be filled by plants that did not manage to make it across the land-bridge in time. When they have been carried across deliberately, many of these plants have made themselves at home as alien invaders. And it is all because of ice-ages and a sudden change in sea-levels, about 6000 years ago.

7

THE ALIENS AWAKEN

How many times have you seen people go out without a coat on sunny days, only to get caught in the rain when the weather changes? Some people never learn. You would think that everyone would know by now that even on hot summer days it is a good idea to carry an umbrella. Our climate is very unreliable.

Plants are a lot smarter than humans when it comes to judging the weather. Imagine what would happen if seeds began to germinate during a few sunny days in mid-winter, or leaves began to sprout after a few warm days in December. Along would come the frost and snow and the new, young growth would be killed.

It takes more than a few bright days to fool most plants because they have developed a useful trick, called **dormancy**. It works like this:

When a seed grows on a plant or a bud develops on a twig, a chemical builds up inside the cells which sends them into a kind of **hibernation**, or winter sleep. All the time the chemical substance is present, the seeds cannot germinate and the buds cannot open.

During winter, freezing temperatures slowly destroy the chemical and by the time spring arrives it has all disappeared, allowing cells to start growing again. It is the plants' safety mechanism, which allows them to survive our cold winters and begin growth again at a time of year when the weather is getting warmer. You can demonstrate how dormancy works with this simple experiment:

How to wake up a cowslip

You will need:
1   Some cowslip seeds (see page 120 for suppliers)
2   Two small flowerpots
3   Two polythene bags, large enough to put the pots in
4   Some potting compost
5   A container with a tight-fitting lid which is large enough
    for one of the flowerpots to fit in

Fill both pots with potting compost and water them. Sow
cowslip seeds on the surface of the wet potting compost,
then put each pot into a polythene bag. Tie the tops with
string. Place one pot on the window-ledge. Put the other
one inside the container, make sure the lid is on tight and
put it in the refrigerator on the top shelf, just under the
freezer compartment. You should tell everyone in your
house that you are doing this, because they will be a bit
surprised if they reach in for the butter and find a pot of
soil lurking amongst the food. If they seem doubtful about
the idea, tell them that the soil is inside a plastic bag and a
sealed container, so nothing nasty will escape into the food.

You will need some patience for this experiment, but
after about two months you should find that hardly any of
the cowslip seeds on the window-ledge have germinated.

On the other hand, if you take the seeds out of the
refrigerator after about six weeks, take the pot out of the
container and stand it on the window-ledge, still in the
polythene bag, all the seeds should germinate in a few days.
If they do not it means they have not had a long enough
cold treatment to awaken them from their winter sleep.
There will still be some dormancy chemical left, stopping
the cells from growing. Put the pot back in the refrigerator
for another couple of weeks and try again if this happens.

If cowslip seeds are sown about a week before they are

HOW TO WAKE UP A COWSLIP

YOU WILL NEED

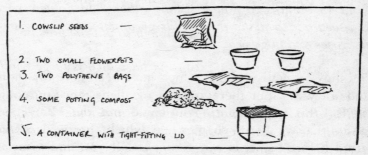

1. COWSLIP SEEDS
2. TWO SMALL FLOWERPOTS
3. TWO POLYTHENE BAGS
4. SOME POTTING COMPOST
5. A CONTAINER WITH TIGHT-FITTING LID

THE EXPERIMENT

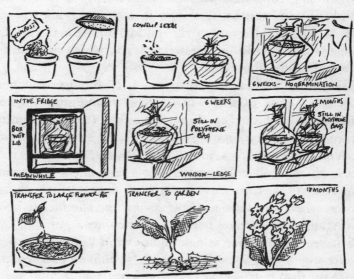

fully ripe they can germinate instantly, but as they ripen the anti-germination chemical begins to build up inside them. Once that happens they will not germinate until they have sat through a long period of cold weather.

Once the seeds germinate and grow two pairs of leaves you should transfer them to flowerpots. Grow them until they are large enough to put in your garden. They will take about 18 months to flower. Many other wild flowers need cold weather to make their seeds germinate, including violets, roses and hogweed.

Cowslips are **native** plants which have been here for thousands of years, but there are lots of aliens that you could use for this experiment. You could use the Himalayan balsam that we met in chapter one, which also needs a cold period before its seeds can germinate. If you find some in late summer, collect the seed and store it in your refrigerator for about two months, then sow it. If you do this you can trick it into waking up in the middle of winter! Another alien that you could use is sweet cicely, which is a garden herb that smells of aniseed.

Lots of plants use this dormancy trick to survive winter, especially **alpine** plants, which grow in mountains where winters are long and icy. Some even need *two* cold winters before they will germinate.

Several types of trees, including birch and sycamore, have seeds which need cold weather to break their dormancy. This means that the seeds do not germinate until the end of winter, when they have a whole spring and summer to grow and establish themselves before winter comes again.

Sycamore is an alien which comes from Europe. You can do an interesting experiment with it that shows exactly where the dormancy chemical is hidden.

Collect two batches of seed in autumn, just as the winged seeds ripen and fall off the tree. Sow one batch straight away in soil. Very carefully peel off the outside of the seed-coat of the others before you plant them. You might need sharp finger-nails for this. You should find that the peeled

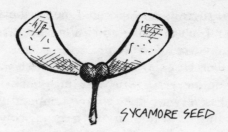

SYCAMORE SEED

sycamore seeds germinate quickly, but the unpeeled ones will not germinate until they have had a long winter chill. This proves that, at least in sycamore, the dormancy chemical is hidden in the seed-coat.

You can try a different kind of dormancy experiment using twigs from trees instead of seeds. In January, cut some twigs from an elder bush and a beech tree and put them in a vase of water on a window-ledge. After about a week or so the elder buds will begin to burst. They have no dormancy mechanism. The beech buds will not burst, however long you wait. Eventually they will just shrivel up and die.

If you do exactly the same experiment in late March, towards the end of winter, you will find that the beech buds will burst too. This is because by March they will then have had enough cold weather to destroy the chemical which is preventing their cells from growing.

So, lots of plants survive winter successfully because they can become dormant. They need cold winters to release their cells from the grip of the dormancy chemical.

One of the predictions of the effect of global warming is that our winters will get warmer. This could be a disaster for plants with dormancy mechanisms. If there is no frost and snow, how will their cells escape from the effects of dormancy chemical? They could sleep for ever, until they eventually die of old age!

Luckily, there is a way out. One of the most important things about living plants and animals is that they are never perfect and never all the same.

Remember Himalayan balsam, the exploding plant from the land of the yeti, which we met back in chapter one? This plant is very sensitive to low temperatures and is killed by frost. But its seeds survive freezing conditions without any problems. They contain the dormancy chemical and need a long period at low temperatures to destroy it all, so that they only germinate and grow once winter has safely passed and the weather gets warmer.

HIMALAYAN BALSAM

Now, you might think that a warm, frost-free winter would be a disaster for a plant like this. Winter might not be long enough or cold enough to wake it up. But it probably has an escape route.

Some Himalayan balsam seeds might have less of the dormancy chemical than others. They could germinate after a shorter period of cold treatment. They would not be such deep sleepers as the usual kind.

In normal winters they might be killed, because they would germinate too soon and then be damaged by late frost. But if winters begin to get warmer they will be able to germinate sooner in safety, and replace the balsams that need a longer cold treatment.

Then, amongst the seeds from the next generation of plants there might be some more seeds which needed an even shorter cold period. Eventually, if this went on year after year, a generation of Himalayan balsam seeds might appear that did not need a winter chill at all. They might replace the deep sleepers completely.

Almost all living plants and animals vary in thousands of tiny details. No two individuals from a single **species** are usually the same unless they are identical twins or unless they are plants grown from cuttings, like the slender speedwell we met back in chapter one.

All this variation is very important. It means that if conditions change, as they are doing now, one of the many varieties might have just the right advantage that will allow it to do better in the new conditions. If all the individuals were identical, they might all die if living conditions got worse.

This is what is known as **natural variation**. Different individuals gain an advantage as conditions change by a process which scientists call **natural selection**.

Natural selection works in favour of the individuals that are best suited to their **environment** and it works against the ones that are not quite as good. It has been going on non-stop since life first began on Earth. Through time, as conditions change, living creatures change as a result of natural selection. The most successful ones multiply, replacing the ones that find the conditions too tough.

When species of plants and animals change over a period of time like this, as a result of natural selection, the process is called **evolution**. It seems more than likely that Himalayan balsam will evolve by natural selection into a new form, which needs fewer cold days before the seeds germinate.

The Strange Case of the Lesser Big-footed Mud Duck

Here is an imaginary example showing how evolution works. The greater small-footed mud ducks live beside the sea, where the sea-shore is made of sloppy mud. They feed on worms, but when they walk out towards the softest mud where the biggest worms are, they sink. They are too heavy and their feet are too small to reach the tastiest worms.

Then, one day, a small duck with big feet is born. Because she has big feet and does not weigh too much, she can walk out on to the very soft mud without sinking into it. When she gets there she has all the big worms to herself. She grows fast and lays lots of eggs. All of her ducklings inherit her small size and big feet. Soon there will be a whole new species, the lesser big-footed mud duck, that can feed on the sloppy mud.

Meanwhile, disaster strikes the greater small-footed mud duck. Global warming melts the glaciers and the sea creeps a bit further up the shore, so all the mud turns sloppy. One by one the greater small-footed mud ducks sink and the lesser big-footed mud duck has the shore to itself.

The scientist who first described the processes of natural selection and evolution was Charles Darwin. He was one of the most famous scientists who ever lived. He had two characteristics which made him a particularly good scientist.

Firstly, he was a very careful observer and took careful notes of everything he discovered. When he was a young man he made a five-year-long voyage around the world on a sailing ship called the *Beagle*. During the voyage he kept detailed notebooks and diaries every day, which he used later to help him describe his theory of evolution.

Secondly, he was curious about everything. He studied barnacles, orchids, pigeons, cats, fossils, climbing plants and countless other forms of life. Once he spent a day playing musical instruments to earthworms, to see which

musical notes they could hear. People must have thought he was mad, but by using his imagination to satisfy his curiosity, he became the greatest biological scientist who ever lived.

We need a few more people like him today. Maybe you could take over where he left off.

8

WHAT IS THIS STUFF CALLED SNOW?

In January 1979, blizzards struck some parts of England. It snowed so hard for several days that by the time the last snowflake settled, the snow-drifts had reached some bedroom window-ledges. Houses in remote areas were cut off for days or even weeks, before bulldozers and snow-ploughs cleared the roads.

That was over ten years ago and most parts of England have not had heavy snow like that since, although Scotland regularly has blizzards in winter. Winter snowfall increases as you go further north, as you get closer to the Arctic Circle, so children in Scotland can rely on getting some snow every year, but for children in Sussex it is something of a rare treat.

Apart from a sudden heavy snowfall in December 1990, which took everyone by surprise, there has been very little snow in England recently. In fact, during the winters of 1987, 1988 and 1989, there was hardly any snow at all, much to the disgust of children who enjoyed sledging, snowballs and making snowmen.

'What is this stuff called snow?' some children were beginning to ask. Now that the world's climate is getting warmer, frost and snow may become even less common in Britain, especially in the southern half of England.

In some ways this will not be such a bad thing. Warmer winters will mean that we will need to spend less money on energy for heating. Travel will be safer and more reliable in winter. In the sudden blizzard in December 1990 hundreds of people were trapped in their cars on roads that crossed high ground. But we would miss cold winters, not just for the fun that snow can bring.

Frost is very important to farmers and gardeners. It kills pests which damage crops. After a mild winter there are always serious outbreaks of pests like greenfly, which survive in large numbers and attack crops early in spring.

Frost also plays a valuable role in breaking down soil into fine particles that are suitable for sowing seeds in. Keen gardeners know that hard frosts can save them a lot of hard work, because they do not have to do so much digging.

The reason for this is that as water freezes it expands and takes up more space. You can prove this by making ice-cubes in the refrigerator. Half-fill the ice-cube tray with water and put it in the freezer compartment. Look at the level again when it has frozen into ice-cubes and you will see that it has risen. As the water froze, it expanded.

Testing the power of ice

When ice expands it pushes against anything around it with enormous force. If you fill a tin with water, put the lid on tight and leave it in the freezer, the ice will push the lid off. Never do this with a glass container, because the expanding

TESTING THE POWER OF ICE

EXPERIMENT

WATER

TIN

FIT LID AND PLACE IN FREEZER

ICE FORCES THE LID OFF
ICE

ice will break it. Freezing water pushes so hard against its surroundings that it can shatter rock.

Gardeners and farmers use this freezing force to help them cultivate the soil. If they dig the soil in autumn and leave the large lumps on the surface, the water held between the tiny soil particles freezes and thaws all winter, pushing the soil particles apart. By spring the big lumps are so weak that they fall apart when you touch them with a rake, making a perfect bed of fine soil for sowing seeds.

So frost can be useful, but it is also the thing that prevents many introduced aliens from escaping into the countryside. We saw in the last chapter that some aliens, like the Himalayan balsam, are easily killed by frost but can survive the winter because their seeds remain dormant.

There are many plants that are not so lucky. These are killed, along with their seeds, at the end of every autumn. For them, frost-free winters will be just what they have been waiting for.

Hardy plants are the ones which will survive winter freezing. All our native biennial and perennial wild flowers are hardy, although many die back temporarily after frost. **Tender** plants are the ones that are killed by frost, like dahlias.

Tough or tender?

You will need:

1 *Some seeds of dahlias, African marigolds or marrows. You can use any of these for this experiment and you can get them from a garden centre, or you can order them from a seed catalogue (see page 119).*
2 *Some paper kitchen towel*
3 *An empty, clean margarine tub*
4 *Some Clingfilm*

Soak the seeds overnight. Line the bottom of the margarine

TOUGH OR TENDER?

YOU WILL NEED

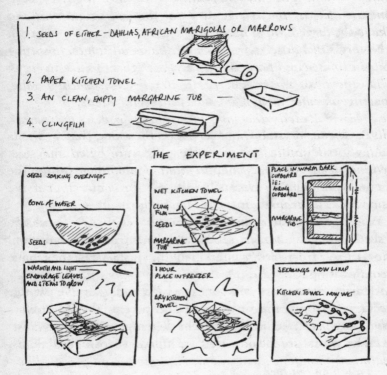

1. SEEDS OF EITHER – DAHLIAS, AFRICAN MARIGOLDS OR MARROWS

2. PAPER KITCHEN TOWEL

3. AN CLEAN, EMPTY MARGARINE TUB —

4. CLINGFILM —

THE EXPERIMENT

SEEDS SOAKING OVERNIGHT

BOWL OF WATER

SEEDS

WET KITCHEN TOWEL

CLING FILM

SEEDS

MARGARINE TUB

PLACE IN WARM DARK CUPBOARD IE: AIRING CUPBOARD

MARGARINE TUB

WARMTH AND LIGHT ENCOURAGE LEAVES AND STEMS TO GROW

1 HOUR PLACE IN FREEZER

DRY KITCHEN TOWEL

SEEDLINGS NOW LIMP

KITCHEN TOWEL NOW WET

tub with paper towel and make it wet. Pour away any water that the towel does not soak up. Now put some soaked seeds in the tub and cover it with Clingfilm. Put the tub in a warm dark place like an airing cupboard. Check every day to see whether the seeds have germinated.

As soon as the roots poke their way out of the seeds transfer the tub to a warm, light place, which will encourage the stems and leaves of the seedlings to grow.

When the seedlings are about three centimetres long, take

them out and replace the wet towel that they are growing on with a dry towel, then put the seedlings back. Replace the Clingfilm and put the margarine tub into the freezing compartment of the refrigerator for about an hour. Then take it out and let them warm up.

Now take a close look. The seedlings will be as limp as boiled cabbage and the towel underneath them will be wet.

This is what happened: the water inside the tiny cells froze. Remember what happened to the tin full of water in the freezer? Exactly the same thing happened to the plant cells, as big ice crystals burst out of them.

All the **cell sap** leaked out. The cells were killed and the seedlings went limp, just like the wilted sunflower seedlings in the experiment in chapter four. All the water that was inside the cells drained out on to the paper.

You could try a few variations on this experiment. Instead of seedlings, put leaves from various plants from the country-side or the garden in the tub. Try using a small shoot from a conifer (these are the trees with spiky leaves, like Christmas trees). Try a moss and also see what happens when you use leaves from house-plants that grow on the window-ledge. I expect that you will find that the conifer needles and the moss show no signs of damage from the cold treatment. Conifers can grow in extremely cold places, like Norway and northern Canada. Mosses can also survive freezing temperatures and often grow in winter, when condi-tions are too cold for most other plants.

You could also try varying the time that you keep seed-lings and leaves in the freezer, to see which can survive low temperatures for the longest. This will tell you which is the hardiest.

Dahlias come from a part of Mexico where there are no frosts. Our cold winters kill them. If winters became warmer because of global warming, exotic plants like dahlias might survive outdoors in some parts of England all through the year. And perhaps they might even spread beyond the garden.

There are already a few places in the British Isles which rarely get frosts in winter, like the Scilly Isles and some parts of Cornwall. It would only take a small rise in average temperatures for many more parts of the country to become frost-free. And that's just what the aliens are waiting for.

9

WIND AND FIRE

On the night of 15 October 1987, one of the most incredible British weather events of the century took place.

As people all over the country watched the weather forecast on their television screens before they went to bed, they heard the weatherman say that a lady had telephoned his office to ask if it was true that a hurricane was on the way. 'Nothing to worry about,' he assured viewers. There were high winds crossing the Atlantic Ocean but they would pass well to the south of the British Isles. Millions of TV viewers switched off their TV sets and went peacefully to bed.

That night, a hurricane struck. By dawn on 16 October fifteen million trees had been blown down, houses had been damaged, greenhouses blown away, cars wrecked and, worst of all, 18 people had been killed. This terrible weather disaster was one of the worst in our island's history.

Since then hurricane-force gales have struck again, although never with such force or with such disastrous results as on that grim October night in 1987. But some scientists believe that as the Earth's atmosphere warms up, catastrophes like the great gale will be a regular feature of our winters.

We saw one reason why this might happen back in chapter three, when Sid the snake was spun around by rising warm air currents. Hot air rises and when this happens cold air is sucked into the space that it leaves behind. This is how winds are often caused.

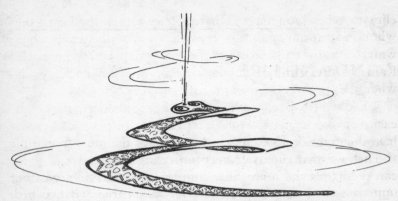

Something that is worrying many scientists about global warming is that it is very hard to predict its effects. Even the largest, most advanced computers cannot predict all of the effects of a few degrees' rise in temperature. And we still do not have enough information to load into the computers, to allow them to make accurate predictions.

One interesting and frightening possibility is that if sea temperatures rise, ocean currents might change direction. Water can store large amounts of heat, so when large volumes of water move around they can suddenly change the climate. A warm current which flows across the Atlantic Ocean towards Scotland, called the North Atlantic Drift, keeps parts of the north-west coast of Britain relatively warm in winter. So warm, in fact, that there are botanic gardens in Western Scotland where they can grow palm trees. If the current moved, so that it missed the British Isles altogether, winters in Scotland would certainly get a lot colder.

In the southern Pacific Ocean a warm current called El Niño reverses direction every few years, usually at around Christmas, causing heavy rain and floods in Peru and Ecuador and leaving hot, dry conditions in Australia.

You can see how the temperature of water can affect

climate when you have a bath. The hot water heats the whole bathroom and fills it with clouds of steam when water vapour condenses in the cold air above the bath. Rain, in the form of condensation, runs down the walls when the steam condenses on cold surfaces.

When warm ocean currents change direction, they can easily change climate. Hot air might rise in places where it has never risen before, generating new winds.

The best that **climatologists** (scientists that study climate) can predict at the moment is that the climate will get more unpredictable, so we should not be surprised if we get hurricanes like the 1987 disaster more often. There was another furious gale, which was not quite as bad, in the early months of 1990.

When people woke up on the morning of 16 October 1987, they could hardly believe their eyes. We are used to seeing the disastrous affects of tropical hurricanes and ty-phoons on television, when they regularly strike tropical areas like Florida, the West Indies and the Philippines. Few people believed that it could happen here.

One of the first things that they noticed was the enormous number of fallen trees littering the landscape. In that single night, more trees blew over than foresters would cut down deliberately in a *whole year*! It was probably the biggest disaster in the history of forests in Britain in the twentieth century. And it has produced some interesting effects.

Take a walk through a deciduous woodland in spring or summer. Deciduous woods are the ones made up of trees like oak, ash or beech, which drop their leaves in winter. Look carefully and you can easily see that the plants are arranged in layers. High above your head the canopy of leaves belonging to the tall forest trees absorbs most of the light, except where there is a gap and sunlight streams through into a woodland glade.

Around you in the woodland are some smaller, younger trees, a few climbing plants like honeysuckle and some shrubs, like wild roses and brambles. Biologists call this the **shrub layer** and it absorbs still more light. Because the light levels are quite low these shrubs often do not flower as well as they would in open areas, where the light is much higher. Honeysuckle rarely flowers in shady woodland but it produces a spectacular display of sweet-scented flowers in sunlit hedgerows.

If you get on your hands and knees you will find yourself down amongst small flowering plants, like bluebells, primroses and wood anemones. In deciduous woodlands they have a neat trick which allows them to grow and flower even though light levels are very low at ground level.

As soon as the first hint of spring appears they put on a spurt of growth and flower very early in the season. By the time that tree leaf buds have burst and the leaf canopy has closed over their heads, they have already produced seeds and are dying down again. Biologists call this the **field** or **herb layer**.

If you lie down on the soil surface of a woodland, to get a worm's eye view, and look closely you will see another layer of plants. These are tiny mosses, which have microscopic leaves and are the oldest of all living plants on the land surface. They covered the ground long before the dinosaurs began to roam the Earth. Most mosses grow best in wet, shady habitats, out of direct sunlight. The damp, shady woodland floor suits them perfectly.

So this was what many woodlands looked like when the gale struck. Imagine the scene in the darkness during that October night in 1987. Up above, the branches of the tree canopy crashed together as shrieking winds tore through them. Broken branches crashed down through the shrub layer and thumped to the ground. The howling gale sent clouds of dry, dead leaves rushing between the tree trunks, which creaked and groaned as the wind lashed their heavy branches. And every now and then, as the gale rose higher,

roots of a tree would give way and it would slowly topple over, like a wounded dinosaur, crashing to the ground and carrying branches of other trees with it. Sometimes there would be a loud crack, as old, weak tree trunks simply snapped in half.

By dawn, when the wind began to die down, many woodlands were devastated. Suddenly, the neat layers that we saw on our walk through the wood were harder to recognize. Fallen trees had left huge gaps in the canopy of branches, letting rays of sunlight through to parts of the forest floor that had not seen sunshine for years.

It seemed like a terrible disaster, especially as famous forests that had taken centuries to develop were severely damaged. But by the following year some people began to think differently.

Where trees had blown over, leaving yawning gaps in the canopy of leaves, seedlings began to germinate. The next generation of trees began to grow, pushing their way upwards to fill the gaps.

In spring spectacular displays of wild flowers appeared, as the higher levels of sunlight reaching the woodland floor allowed the field layer to flower better than ever before.

The same thing happened to the shrub layer in summer, when brambles, honeysuckle and wild roses bloomed, producing masses of fruits that animals could eat in the autumn.

Meanwhile the fallen branches began to rot away. Fungi moved in, eating away at the wood and producing colourful crops of toadstools. When the wood rotted, small animals like beetles, centipedes and spiders crept into its cavities and set up home. For many of the plants and animals that lived on the woodland floor, the great gale was probably the best thing that ever happened to them.

In some forests the fallen trees were quickly cleared away and new ones were planted. When this happens it leaves behind a large amount of bare ground, where weeds can grow. It also creates opportunities for alien plants.

There are several aliens that live in our forests already. One is a moss from South Africa, which has the tongue-twisting name *Orthodontium lineare*. Very few mosses have common names and most are only known by their scientific, Latin names. *Orthodontium* is a beautiful little plant which grows in dense emerald-green cushions, covered with little capsules on curved stalks.

Mosses are very good at moving around, because they produce tiny spores, which are like microscopic seeds. These are so small and light that they can be carried for miles on the wind, before they settle on a wet surface, germinate and grow into a new moss plant.

Another woodland alien is New Zealand willow-herb, a tiny, creeping plant that often grows along the edges of woodland footpaths, especially in northern Britain. You have probably seen its tall cousin, the rose-bay willow-herb, which colonizes waste ground and newly felled woodlands.

NEW ZEALAND
WILLOW-HERB

It produces masses of purple flowers in late summer. All willow-herbs have small seeds fitted with a tiny parachute, which allows them to drift into new habitats on the breeze. They are all very efficient colonizers of bare ground and we already have at least four alien species of willow-herb in Britain.

So some aliens have already moved into our woodlands.

Perhaps gales like the 1987 disaster, together with a warmer climate in summer, will allow a few more to follow them and colonize bare areas left by fallen trees. We can only wait and watch.

Now, several years after the great gale, the holes in the woodland canopies are beginning to fill in again. The shoots of green plants always grow towards the light and the young trees in the woodland shrub layer are growing up towards the level of the older trees. You can show how plants react to light with this simple experiment.

Struggling towards the light

You will need:
1 *A small seed tray*
2 *Some soil*
3 *Some sunflower seeds*
4 *A small cardboard box that will fit over the seed tray*
Fill the seed tray with soil and sow the sunflower seeds.

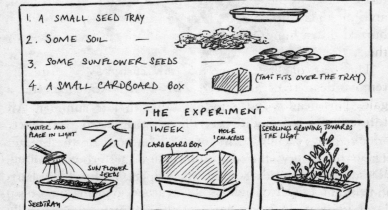

STRUGGLING TOWARDS THE LIGHT

YOU WILL NEED

1. A SMALL SEED TRAY
2. SOME SOIL   —
3. SOME SUNFLOWER SEEDS   —
4. A SMALL CARDBOARD BOX   (THAT FITS OVER THE TRAY)

THE EXPERIMENT

WATER AND PLACE IN LIGHT
SUNFLOWER SEEDS
SEED TRAY

1 WEEK
CARDBOARD BOX
HOLE 1 CM ACROSS

SEEDLINGS GROWING TOWARDS THE LIGHT

Keep them well watered and leave them in a warm place until the first shoots just begin to show above the soil. Cut a small hole, about 1cm. across, in the bottom of your box and then turn it upside down over the tray of seedlings. Leave it for about a week then take a look underneath, and you will see all the seedlings, with long spindly stems, growing towards the hole where the light is coming through.

Once the seedling trees reach the forest canopy they will fill in the gaps, so that much less sunlight will reach the woodland floor. Then the woodland will return to the way it was before the gale and the carpet of wildflowers in spring will not be so spectacular – until the next gale strikes!

Fire is the hazard that foresters fear most. Forest fires are very difficult to control, especially when trees are planted close together, and they can do millions of pounds' worth of damage. They are not very common in Britain, but in hotter countries they are a constant problem. In 1990 there were terrible fires in the south of France, during a long drought, and in 1983 there were fires in South Australia which burned down hundreds of houses and threatened to destroy the city of Adelaide.

The fear of fire is one of the reasons why foresters remove dead trees and clear away fallen branches after a gale. This dead wood is an extra fire risk. If you visit any forest during a drought you will see signs posted everywhere which warn you not to light fires.

Fire has also been a major problem on moorlands in long, hot summers like those of 1989 and 1990. **Moorland** often consists of a layer of plants, like heather, growing on a deep layer of peat. In some parts of the country, like the hilly

Pennines, gamekeepers burn away the heather at regular intervals during winter, when the peat is wet. The fire quickly burns away the old heather branches but the wet peat prevents damage to the roots. This allows the heather to produce succulent new shoots for birds like grouse to feed on.

Although careful burning of heather in winter helps wildlife on moorlands, an accidental fire in summer is a disaster. Peat is made from the remains of dead plants and when it dries out it burns very easily. In some countries, like Ireland, they use it instead of coal to heat houses.

It only needs someone to drop a cigarette or knock over a camping stove and a fire will start that will burn away all the surface plants and burn down into the peat for days on end. By the time the fire goes out, nothing is left alive.

It seems certain that we can expect more forest and moorland fires if global warming makes summers hotter and warmer, like those of 1989 and 1990. This means that people will have to take much more care not to start fires in the countryside and it also means that footpaths across moorland and through forests will often be closed when the fire risk is high.

When fires do happen, the bare, burnt soil that is left behind is quickly colonized by plants. Rose-bay willow-herb, which we met earlier, grows particularly well on soil that has been scorched by fire. So well, in fact, that in America, where it is a serious problem, it is called fireweed.

10

GOOD GRIEF!
IT'S A JUNGLE OUT THERE!

Although global warming could cause changes in the climate which will mean that drought will become more of a problem for plants, it will bring them some benefits too. Carbon dioxide (CO_2) is one of the main causes of the greenhouse effect. But, as we saw in chapter two, it is also the raw material that plants use for growth.

Plants absorb CO_2 gas through their leaves and absorb water and dissolved **minerals** from the soil through their roots. These basic ingredients are all that they need to make more cells, so that they can grow.

If the climate becomes warmer and there is more CO_2 in the air, they will grow faster. You can show that this will happen using a simple trick with pondweed.

We saw in chapter two that when plants use CO_2 for growth, they release oxygen (O_2) into the air. The more CO_2 they use, the more O_2 they release. Normally we cannot see oxygen, because it is a colourless gas, but water plants give off a stream of bubbles of oxygen as they grow. (This is why you should put pondweed in fish tanks – the oxygen bubbles that they give off help to keep fish healthy.) If we measure how fast they produce O_2 bubbles, we can see how fast they are using CO_2. And if we find that they are using more CO_2, we can be sure that they are growing faster.

Here is an experiment to prove that plants can grow better if they are given more CO_2:

The plant bubble machine

You will need:

1 *Some pondweed. You may be able to find some in a pond. If not, visit your local pet shop. They sell pondweed for fish tanks.*
2 *A clear plastic two-litre bottle, with the top cut off. Fill the bottle with tap water.*
3 *Some bicarbonate of soda. You can buy this in a supermarket, where you will find it on the shelf next to the flour*

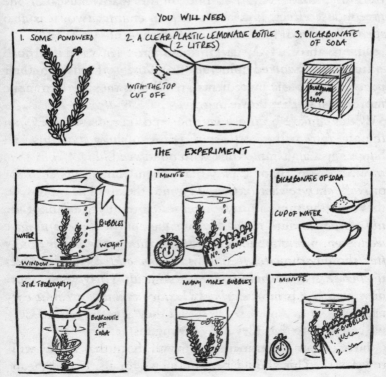

and yeast. People use it for making scones. You can also get it from chemist shops.

Cut the top off the bottle with scissors. Cut a piece of pondweed about 15cm. long and tie a small weight to the cut end, so that it sinks to the bottom of the tall plastic bottle.

Stand the bottle on a sunny window-ledge and leave it for about half an hour. Then look at the cut end of the stem. You should see a stream of bubbles forming and rising to the surface.

These are bubbles of pure oxygen gas, made when the plant uses the CO_2 which is dissolved in the water. Count how many bubbles are produced in a minute and write the number down. If you want to be scientifically accurate, repeat this two or three times and work out the average.

Now dissolve a teaspoon of bicarbonate of soda in a few centimetres of water in the bottom of a cup. It will fizz a bit and some of it may not dissolve. (Did you know that the 'fizz' in lemonade is really dissolved carbon dioxide too?)

When the fizzing dies down, pour the dissolved bicarbonate of soda into the bottle with the water weed and give it a stir. Try not to pour in the undissolved sludge from the bottom of the cup, or it may make the water cloudy so that you will not be able to see the bubbles.

After about five minutes count the number of oxygen bubbles per minute released from the end of the cut pondweed stem. There is more carbon dioxide in the water now, after the bicarbonate of soda has been added, so you will see that lots more bubbles are produced. This proves that when a plant has more carbon dioxide available it can use it faster.

So more carbon dioxide in the air will mean that plants will grow faster. This should be good news for us. It will mean that crop plants will produce more food, to feed more people.

But no one knows for sure what effect all this will have on plants in the garden and the countryside. Will all plants grow faster or will some make better use of the extra CO_2? We can be quite sure that some plants will benefit more than others, but we will have to wait and see which ones these will be.

Most plants grow very slowly. Because we cannot actually see them moving it is sometimes difficult to believe that they are really growing in competition with one another at all.

If we made a video film of plants growing in a roadside verge during a single summer and then played it back at several hundred times its normal speed, we would then see how they really behave. It would remind you of a rugby scrum, or of the dinner queue at school when the teachers are not watching. We would see the plants pushing and shoving, struggling for light and space. Some would be shaded out by taller plants and die away, others would form a dense canopy of leaves and dominate shorter plants.

And all this is just on the surface. Below the ground the roots are behaving in the same way, forcing their way through the soil and trying to reach water.

Measuring competition between plants is not easy, because it often takes weeks or months for the effects to appear. You cannot say what is happening by just looking. You need to make regular measurements over a period of time.

Scientists who investigate interactions between different kinds of living organisms and their surroundings are called **ecologists**. They often use a simple piece of equipment which is designed to allow them to sample populations of plants. This is called a **quadrat**. You can make one by joining together four short canes, each 60cm. long, to form a 50cm. square, like the one in the drawing below. You can bind the corners

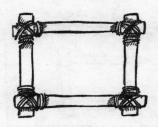

together with tough string or wire. This is all the equipment you need to find out how plants behave when they are crowded together or when they are short of light, water or warmth.

Try this simple experiment to find out what kind of conditions suit daisies in lawns.

Down among the daisies

For this experiment you will need to find an area of mown grass which has daisies in it, like a lawn or a playing field.

You also need to find an area which is shaded and an area where the grass is regularly trampled.

Lay your quadrat down in each of these areas and see how much of the area is covered with daisies. You can do this most easily using a five-point scale:

Score 1 for no daisies
  2 for less than a quarter (25%) of the area covered by daisies
  3 for half (50%) of the area covered by daisies
  4 for more than three-quarters (75%) of the area covered by daisies
  5 for all daisies

DOWN AMONG THE DAISIES

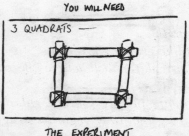

YOU WILL NEED

3 QUADRATS —

THE EXPERIMENT

AREA OF MOWN GRASS

AREA OF TRAMPLED GRASS

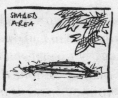

SHADED AREA

1. = NO DAISIES. 2. = 25% DAISIES. 3. = 50% DAISIES. 4. 75% DAISIES. 5. = ALL DAISIES

Make three sets of measurements in each area and work out the average of the scores for each.

Draw your results out in a bar graph, which will probably look something like this:

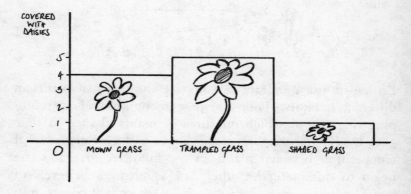

This shows you that:

1 Daisies do not like growing in shade
2 They grow particularly well where the soil is trampled and disturbed

Daisies like growing in grass that is regularly mowed. If the grass is allowed to grow, they begin to struggle to compete with it.

You can prove this by finding an area with plenty of daisies and marking out a 50cm. square with four wooden pegs, to make what ecologists call a **permanent quadrat**. Make sure that the grass is allowed to grow in and around your permanent quadrat for the summer. Then compare the scores for the area covered by daisies in mown parts of the lawn and your permanent quadrat. You will find that daisies are poor competitors compared with grass. As the grass grows taller they will begin to disappear.

A PERMANENT QUADRAT .

DAISIES ARE POOR COMPETITORS AS THEY DISAPPEAR WHEN
THE GRASS GROWS TALL

Ecologists use quadrats to compare the types of plants in different habitats. They use permanent quadrats to compare the way in which mixtures of plants change as time goes by. The change could be due to different amounts of competition between plants in the mixture, so that some begin to dominate the others, or to changes in levels of light, warmth or water. As global warming comes into effect, ecologists will be using permanent quadrats to show how hotter, drier summers and warmer, wetter winters are affecting our plant life.

We only need to look around us to see that some plants are very good competitors. After the great gale in 1987, for example, sycamore seedlings began to appear in woodlands that had been dominated by oak and beech trees that were blown down by the wind.

Sycamore is an alien. It was introduced into this country quite recently, probably sometime between AD 1500 and 1600. In 1588, when Sir Francis Drake defeated the Spanish Armada and Elizabeth I was Queen, it was still a rare tree in England.

It comes from the mountains of central Europe and produces lovely white wood that was once used for making equipment for dairies. It is a good timber tree, grows fast and is very tough. But it has one major fault: it enjoys life here too much. Each tree produces thousands of winged seeds, which spin like helicopter rotor blades as they drop

from the branches. This slows down their fall to earth, so that they can be carried quite long distances on the wind.

If you stand on a hilltop on a windy day and throw the 'helicopters' into the air, you can check how well they work by measuring how far away they fall to earth.

With its spinning seeds, sycamore has spread to most parts of the British Isles in the space of only 400 years. It even grows in the coldest, windiest areas.

It is becoming quite a problem plant, because it grows so fast and releases so many seeds that it produces woodlands where we do not need them. Once the seeds invade grassland they quickly turn it into woodland. Then the grassland flowers underneath are hidden in dense shade and die out.

People have to spend a lot of time, money and effort removing sycamore from places where it is not wanted, like nature reserves. It is one of the few trees that have become weeds.

This just goes to show how easily these aliens can take over. Once a sycamore tree gets into a woodland, it produces seeds year after year, ready to take over the woodland when other trees are blown down or die.

Sycamore has another interesting feature which makes it a successful competitor. When alien plants arrive they often leave their natural enemies behind. It usually takes a long time for new pests and diseases to learn to live on aliens, so to begin with they can grow in safety, free from enemies.

Very few pests feed on sycamore. There is one fungus, called tar spot fungus, which grows on its leaves. It makes ugly black circles all over their upper surfaces. This damages the leaves but does no permanent damage to the tree.

At the last count there were only about 16 different kinds of insect feeding on sycamore. This is a tiny number. Birch trees are eaten by about 280 different kinds of insect and oak trees act as food for more that 320 different types.

So when global warming takes hold, we cannot tell which plants will grow fastest. But we do know that the aliens that arrive here will have very few natural enemies to keep them in control. So if they like our new climate, they may begin to take over. They only have one enemy that might stop them: us.

11

CLOSE ENCOUNTERS
OF THE ALIEN KIND

You have nearly reached the end of your experiments. You have seen how clouds form, rain falls and wind blows. You have shown how plants are very sensitive to tiny changes in their surroundings and how they are affected by gales, heat, drought, cold, ice, fire and flood. You have seen how they compete with one another for water and light. So now you can use this information to make some predictions.

If the greenhouse effect does change our climate, we can be certain that some plants will be winners and some will be losers. Some plants that are growing in the countryside now will find the new conditions more to their liking and begin to spread. Others will find the going too tough and slowly disappear from the scene.

And somewhere in between these, there are aliens, waiting for their chance.

You have met some well established aliens already but

there are plenty more lurking in some surprising places. Some have been here so long and are mixed in with the local plants so well that most people think they have been here for ever.

Take ground elder, for example. This is a terrible weed, with stems that creep under the soil. If you try to dig it up, every tiny piece that you leave behind in the soil will grow into a new plant. Gardeners have been trying to get rid of it for years, without much success.

But the funny thing is that, like most aliens, ground elder was introduced into Britain deliberately. The Romans brought it with them from Europe, as a vegetable to eat!

No one wants ground elder now, as it tastes *disgusting*, but it has had some uses. It is another one of those confusing plants

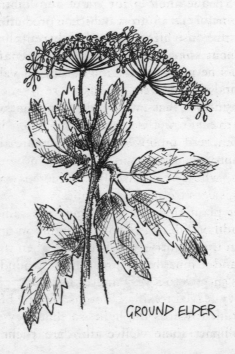

GROUND ELDER

with several different common names, but all scientists call it by its scientific Latin name, which is *Aegopodium podagraria*. This name tells you a lot about the plant if you understand Latin, because Aegopodium means 'poorly foot' and podagraria means 'gout'. There is an interesting story about that.

In some parts of England ground elder used to be called goutweed and in other areas it was sometimes called bishops' weed. Several hundred years ago people believed that ground elder would cure gout, which causes legs and feet to swell up. Plants like this, which were useful as medicines, were grown in herb gardens, often near churches and cathedrals. So it might have become a weed in bishops' gardens and perhaps this is how it got its other common name, bishops' weed.

When a new alien plant arrives it often has trouble finding somewhere to grow which is not already occupied by other plants which have been here for much longer. Several aliens, like wallflowers, have been forced to put down roots between bricks and stones in walls, where few other plants will survive.

The wallflower was introduced from southern Europe so long ago that no one is exactly sure when it arrived, but birds which feed on its seed pods soon carried its sticky seeds up into the crevices in walls. It is now quite common on castles, where it has easily conquered walls that withstood long sieges from mighty armies.

Another plant that has performed the same trick is ivy-leaved toadflax, which is also very common on almost every old wall in the country. We do know when this one arrived – 1617 – and it must have spread itself around very quickly. It owes its success to a very interesting trick.

When ivy-leaved toadflax blooms, its tiny blue and yellow flowers point towards the light, so that they attract insects which pollinate them. Once they are pollinated and the seeds begin to develop, the seed capsules, which are on long stalks, turn around and grow away from the light, into dark crevices in the wall. So ivy-leaved toadflax actually plants its own seeds in the wall. No wonder it does so well there. You can see how it grows for yourself:

The alien that hides its seeds

In spring or early summer, find a small ivy-leaved toadflax plant in a wall and transfer it into a pot of soil. Water it well while it settles into its new surroundings, then stand it on a sunny window-ledge. After a few weeks it will produce flowers, which will point towards the light, then once these die the seed capsules will quickly begin to bend away from the light and hide behind the flowerpot.

THE ALIEN THAT HIDES ITS SEEDS

Walls are usually very hot, dry places and these aliens that have colonized them can survive with very little water. A hotter, drier climate should allow them to spread into other dry habitats, where less tough plants will die out.

Even invading water plants will benefit from more warmth. Wet habitats, like rivers, ponds and canals have had their share of alien invaders in the past. In the future, if water becomes warmer in summer and freezes less often in winter, we may well see more aliens in our waterways. Past experience tells us that once they arrive, they can spread very fast.

The most famous example of a floating alien was Canadian pondweed, a plant that was introduced into a lake at Duns Castle in Berwickshire, near the border of England and Scotland, in 1842. Five years later it had spread to a reservoir in Leicestershire, in the centre of England. No one is quite sure how it managed to travel so far, so quickly. Perhaps a duck carried a bit of the weed on its foot.

At that time, before railways were common, industrial goods were carried around England by barges along canals. Before long, Canadian pondweed got into a canal in Leicestershire.

It could not have chosen a better place to start, because Leicestershire was the centre of the whole canal system. As barges sailed through the weed they broke it into little pieces and dragged it along with them, until it had spread everywhere and choked waterways all over the country.

Another floating alien is the water fern, yet another arrival from North America. It was introduced into ornamental ponds here in 1910 and quickly started exploring new,

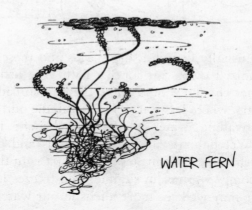

WATER FERN

wet habitats. This is a pretty little plant which could quite easily be carried on ducks' feet. It turns bright red in autumn and is often damaged by long, cold winters. Cold conditions may have kept it at bay up until now, but if they get warmer we can expect it to become more common.

A warmer climate will give invaders that have escaped into the countryside a helping hand. It will also give some new garden plants the opportunity to explore the world beyond the garden fence.

If you want to investigate which ones might be about to break out, visit your local garden centre. This is where most of tomorrow's alien invaders are lurking, waiting for some unsuspecting gardeners to buy them, take them home and look after them. Once they are comfortably established in the flower-beds they will grow, flower, produce seeds and wait for conditions to change. When this happens and other plants begin to retreat, their day will come.

Take a long, hard look at the rows of seed packets in the racks. Amongst them you will find several varieties of snapdragons. You probably know these flowers well, because they have flowers like a bulldog's jaws, which yawn

SNAPDRAGON

open when you squeeze their sides gently and then snap shut when you let go.

Snapdragons have already taken a few cautious steps out of the garden into the wide world beyond. Look around in towns and you may find them growing on old walls or between cracks in pavements. They have tiny seeds, which are shaken out of the seed pods like pepper from a pepper-pot. They quite often stick to birds' feet or gardeners' shoes and get carried far away from their place in the flower garden.

Snapdragons grow wild in Mediterranean countries. Some climatologists believe that by the middle of the next century parts of southern England will have a climate like the Mediterranean. That will suit snapdragons very well. They can already survive our milder winters without much damage. When the greenhouse effect creates warmer winters they should do very well here.

A bit further along the rack you will find sweet-williams, which originally come from eastern Europe but have already hopped over the garden wall in many places in Britain. The more our climate comes to resemble that of Yugoslavia and Greece, the more sweet-williams will like it.

SWEET-WILLIAM

If you look amongst the small potted plants for the flower border, you may find a little plant with greeny-grey,

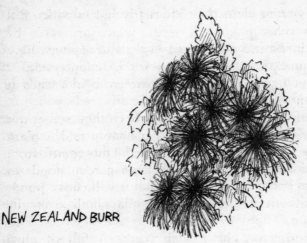

NEW ZEALAND BURR

fern-like leaves, called New Zealand burr. It has another tongue-twister of a Latin name – *Acaena microphylla*. This has spiky little seeds which stick in your socks and can get transported all over the place in the fur of animals. As you can guess from the name, it comes from New Zealand.

It also grows in Australia and it has been here before, carried to Britain in imported sheep's wool. It has escaped around a few woollen mills which were used to process the wool. If it becomes more popular in gardens we can expect to see it a lot more often in dry habitats in the countryside.

Move along through the garden centre to the area where the trees and shrubs are and you will probably find some *Rosa rugosa*. This is a tough rose from Japan with large, sweet-smelling flowers and very large rose hips. It is quite popular as a plant for hedges and there are lots of varieties.

Rosa rugosa might be pretty, but it is a real thug of a plant. Like a lot of plant invaders, it creeps along with underground stems, then produces thick, prickly shoots which are strong enough to lift paving stones and spear through asphalt roads and drives. Because it is so tough, town councils often plant it beside roads and in parks. But like so many other plants, its seeds, which are eaten by animals and birds and distributed in their droppings, have already germinated in some places in the countryside. It could turn out to be a prickly customer to deal with if it gets out of control.

Now take a look in the section where they sell water plants, for garden ponds. You will probably find a plant called swamp stonecrop for sale there. This comes from Australia and has begun to escape from garden ponds in Britain. Ecologists are very worried that it will choke ponds and push out native plants in wet places all over the country.

Look around you. The garden centre is full of alien plants. And the people that are buying them do not suspect that by giving them a home in their gardens, they may be unleashing a reign of terror in the countryside sometime in the future. You have got to warn them!

Ask them to examine their socks for New Zealand burrs! Tell them to treat their *Rosa rugosa* with great suspicion! Tell them the terrible tale of Japanese knotweed! Remind them what happened when gardeners grew *Rhododendron ponticum* and slender speedwell!

They will not listen, of course. They are already in the

grip of the aliens, bewitched by their pretty flowers and leaves, overwhelmed by the scent of their blooms. All the aliens have to do is to sit there, looking pretty, and they know that one of these helpless human gardeners will pick them up and plant them.

Instead, the customers in the garden centre will probably go to the check-out counter and complain to the owner that there is a crazy kid following them around. It is always the same when scientists warn the world about dangers ahead. Nobody listens. Until it is too late. Nobody believes that there is anything to worry about. But if you have done the experiments, you will know the truth!

SCIENTIFIC TERMS

Alien
When it is used in this book, this word means a plant that comes from a foreign country and which does not naturally grow in Britain.

Allergic
A reaction that some people have to certain materials or chemicals. Some people are allergic to certain kinds of plants and their skin comes up in bumps if they touch them. Some people are allergic to pollen and suffer from **hay fever**.

Alpine
Alpine plants grow in mountainous regions, where the winter weather is very severe and summers are short. They can survive freezing temperatures for long periods.

Annuals
These are plants that grow, flower, produce **seeds** and die in a single year. Lots of weeds are annuals.

Atmosphere
The atmosphere is the air above us. At ground level it is made mainly of the gases **oxygen**, nitrogen and **carbon dioxide**, mixed with **water vapour**. As you go higher above the Earth, the amount of oxygen in the air gets less, so pilots of high-flying aeroplanes have to breathe oxygen from bottles. The outermost layer of the atmosphere is the stratosphere, which finishes at about 50 kilometres above the Earth.

Average

You need to work out the average to see how one group of living things differs from another. If you take a series of individual measurements of any living things, like the height of your friends in your class, you will find that they vary quite a lot. Some people will be tall, some people will be short. Some people in the next class up, who are older than you, might be shorter than you are. And some younger people in the next class down might be taller than you are, even though they are younger. So where in the scale do you fit in?

The way to find out is to work out the average height of children of your own age in your class. You do this by adding all the heights together and dividing by the number of people in your class. This will give you the average height, taking into account people that are taller or shorter than is normal for their age. You can check whether you are above or below average height for your age.

This is a very useful way of comparing groups of plants, to see if any of the individuals are very different from the rest of the group.

Bar chart

This is a way of showing differences in a series of measurements as a picture. Instead of just writing down the numbers, you draw vertical bars instead. The bigger the number, the longer the bar. It lets you see very quickly what is going on.

Biennials

Plants that **germinate** and grow into a leafy plant in the first year, then sit through winter without doing much, then grow again and produce flowers in the second year. Then they die.

Botanist
A scientist who studies plants.

Carbon
Carbon is the most important substance on Earth and is the basic material that all living organisms are built from. Coal and diamonds are made of carbon too. Its chemical symbol is C.

Carbon dioxide
This is the gas which is made when **carbon** burns in **oxygen**. Its chemical formula is CO_2. It is one of the most important gases that cause the **greenhouse effect**.

Cells
All living organisms are made of cells, which are the basic building blocks that their bodies are constructed from. A typical plant cell is about one tenth of a millimetre across – too small to see without a powerful magnifying glass.

Cell sap
The juice that fills plant cells. If the cell sap leaks the cells collapse and a plant **wilts**.

Climate
Our climate is created by the weather conditions that exist in our part of the world. Britain has a cool, wet climate. The Amazon has a warm, wet climate. The Sahara has a hot, dry climate. The Arctic has a cold, dry climate.

Climatologist
A scientist who studies the weather and the effects that it has on us.

Condensation
Condensation happens when **water vapour** carried in warm air touches a cold surface. When the air cools the water vapour turns to liquid droplets. Clouds are made of condensed water vapour.

Dormancy
Seeds which cannot **germinate** immediately after they are
shed by a plant are said to be dormant. Some seeds need a
cold chill to overcome this dormancy. Seeds which are
dormant can often live for a long time in the soil before
they germinate.

Ecologist
A scientist who studies the ways in which plants and animals
interact with each other.

Ecosystem
When a group of plants and animals live together and depend
on one another they form an ecosystem. Often, they feed on
one another. A pond is a good example of an ecosystem, full
of plants and animals that are always found together.

Environment
The conditions that living organisms exist in. These can be
a combination of temperature, moisture, wind, sunshine,
soil conditions and levels of pollution.

Evolution
The way in which animals or plants gradually change over
long periods of time, so that they can survive in a changing
environment.

Extinct
The word used to describe a type of plant or animal that
has completely disappeared from the Earth. Dinosaurs and
dodos are extinct. Once an animal or plant is extinct, it will
never reappear.

Field layer
The layer of small plants, less than half a metre tall, which
grow in woodlands. **Herb layer** means the same thing.
Herbs are small plants.

Germination
When **seeds** get wet their **cells** take in water and swell up. This bursts the outer coat of the seed and the baby plant inside begins to grow, using up food reserves that are stored in the seed when it is made on the plant.

Glacier
Glaciers are massive rivers of ice that are formed in mountainous places where it is very cold. They melt or grow, depending on whether the weather becomes warmer or colder.

Global warming
An increase in **average** temperatures, measured over the course of a year, which is taking place all over the planet, because the **greenhouse effect** is getting stronger.

Graph
A picture which shows how measurements change as time goes by.

Greenhouse effect
When the Sun's rays strike the Earth's surface it heats up. The earth releases this heat again but a lot of it is trapped by gases in the **atmosphere**, which prevent the heat from escaping back into outer space. The greenhouse effect keeps the Earth warm, but now that it is getting stronger the Earth might get too warm, if we are not careful.

Greenhouse gases
These are the gases that trap heat and cause the **greenhouse effect**. Most of the pollutants that humans put into the **atmosphere** are greenhouse gases, which are making the greenhouse effect too strong, causing **global warming**. This is why we are trying to cut down on the release of **carbon dioxide**, which is a powerful greenhouse gas.

Habitat
This is the name given to the type of **ecosystem** that a plant or animal is usually found in. The habitat of frogs is a pond, the habitat of squirrels is in a forest and the habitat of children is in front of television sets!

Hardy
The word used by gardeners to describe plants that are not killed by frost and snow.

Hay fever
Some people are **allergic** to pollen. When they breathe it in, it makes their eyes water and they cannot stop sneezing. This is the commonest type of allergy.

Herb layer
This means the same as **field layer**.

Hibernation
The word used to describe how animals sleep over the winter, when there is no food and conditions are too cold for them. Bats and hedgehogs hibernate. **Dormancy** is the word used to describe the same thing in plants. Buds and **seeds** are often dormant through the winter.

Ice-age
In the past, the Earth has regularly warmed up and cooled down. When it cools down enormous sheets of ice spread outwards from the North and South Poles and down from high mountains. The last ice-age finished about 9000 years ago. This country has been completely covered in ice several times in the far distant past. Ice-ages drive out or kill all the plants and animals.

Latin
Latin is the written language that the Romans used. No one actually speaks it any more in everyday conversation, but

scientists use it to name plants and animals. Every scientist in the world understands what Latin names for living organisms mean.

Microscope

Microscopes are pieces of scientific equipment with powerful lenses, which magnify very small things. Some can magnify over 1000 times. You need these to see very small objects. If you magnified a plant cell 1000 times it would still only be ten centimetres long.

Minerals

These are elements that are formed in the Earth, like iron (chemical symbol Fe), nitrogen (chemical symbol N) and phosphorus (chemical symbol P). Many of them are important for plant growth.

Moorland

An **ecosystem** that forms on hills, where the **climate** is often cold and wet and where the summers are short. Heather is one of the commonest plants on moorlands, because it can grow in these harsh conditions. There are often peat bogs on moorlands.

Native

A native plant is one that has always grown in a particular country and has not been deliberately or accidentally introduced by humans.

Natural selection

The way in which plants or animals that are most comfortable in any particular **environment** tend to multiply and replace similar plants and animals that find the conditions too tough. In other words, the living things that tend to be best equipped to live in the environment usually survive and increase.

Natural variation
All living things vary in tiny details. We humans can only recognize each other because we each differ in things like height, hair colour and eye colour. Every individual human being is different from every other, unless they are identical twins. If you look hard enough, you will find variation between almost all living things of the same type, or **species**.

Oasis
There is some water even in the driest deserts. It often comes from wells or rare natural springs which bubble to the surface. Wherever there is water, plants can be grown, so around wells there are dense patches of lush vegetation, surrounded by desert. Each of these islands of greenery in a sea of sand is called an oasis.

Ovules
These are the tiny eggs inside a flower, which eventually grow into **seeds**, after they have been fertilized by a **pollen** grain.

Oxygen
Oxygen is the gas that we breathe. Its chemical symbol is O and the chemical formula for oxygen is O_2. It is made by plants, which release it into the **atmosphere**.

Peat
The remains of dead plants, that pile up on top of each other in layers. If you dig down through the layers, it is like taking a journey back through time. Peat takes thousands of years to form and is found in peat bogs, which are like massive wet sponges, because they absorb a lot of water. Dried peat is sometimes burned as a fuel.

Perennials
Plants that grow and flower year after year. All trees and shrubs are perennials.

Permanent quadrat
A fixed area of land which is marked out, so that you can see how the mixture of plants and animals on the land changes as time goes by.

Pith cells
Big, spongy **cells** that you find in the middle of stems.

Pollen
Tiny **cells**, like dust, that are released from flowers and which fertilize the eggs, or **ovules**, in other flowers. Pollen is often carried on the wind or by insects, like bees and butterflies, which visit flowers.

Potometer
A piece of scientific equipment for measuring the amount of water that plants use.

Predator
A predator is a living thing (usually an animal) which depends on killing and eating other living things for its food supply. Cheetahs, for example, are predators which feed on gazelles. Ladybirds are predators which feed on greenfly.

Quadrat
A square frame, used for enclosing areas of land which you want to compare with other similar areas of land, so that you can see what is happening to the plants and animals in them.

Radiate
Warm objects radiate heat. Your skin radiates heat, passing it on to the air, so that you do not overheat. The Earth radiates heat too.

Radioactive
Radioactive elements change from one form to another as

time passes, giving out radioactivity as they change. Radioactivity is often very dangerous for humans. Too much of it can kill you, but it also has important uses in medicine.

Radio-carbon dating

Radioactive elements change from one form to another at a steady rate, so if you know how fast this happens and you can measure how much radioactivity an object contains, it is often possible to work out very accurately how old it is, even if it is tens of thousands of years old.

Rain forest

A wet, steamy tropical forest where the air is so full of **water vapour** that everything is permanently damp. These forests are an important **habitat** for many of the most unusual animals on Earth and contain more kinds of living organism than any other habitat on land.

Sap

The mixture of water and sugar which is carried around plants in the tiny pipes that run through their stems and leaves.

Seeds

A seed is a tiny plant, surrounded by a food store and a tough, protective coat, which can be carried around by wind, animals, or water. When it lands in a suitable place, it will **germinate**.

Shrub layer

The layer of small trees and shrubs, up to about two metres tall, which you find in woodlands.

Species

This is the general word which biologists use when they talk about different types of animals. For example, thrushes, robins and blackbirds are all different species of bird. Daisies, buttercups and bluebells are all different species of flower.

Sporopollenin
An incredibly tough material that coats the outside of **pollen** grains. Even when pollen has been buried for thousands of years the sporopollenin coat is undamaged. The sporopollenin coat has a pattern which is different for each **species** of plant.

Starch
An important material that plants store in their **cells**. It is made from the sugar that plants make from **carbon dioxide**.

Stigma
The part of the flower where **pollen** grains land and grow, until they reach the egg **cells**, or **ovules**.

Stomata
Tiny pores in the surface of leaves, which let **carbon dioxide** in and let **oxygen** escape.

Tap-roots
Deep, strong roots that grow down into the depths of the soil, where there is always water. Carrots are tap-roots.

Tender
The word that gardeners use to describe plants that are killed by frost.

Water vapour
When water gets hot, it turns into an invisible gas called water vapour. When this **condenses** it turns into clouds and then rain.

Weeds
Plants that grow in places where they become a nuisance, usually because they interfere with crops.

Wilt
The way that plants collapse when their **cells** dry out.

Xylem tubes
The microscopic pipes inside a plant which transport water around from one place to another.

SUPPLIERS

• Microscopes and magnifiers

Early Learning Centres, which are in many towns and cities (look for the Toy Shops section in the Yellow Pages telephone directory), stock several different types of magnifier and microscope. The most useful is the Tasco pocket microscope, which has a built-in light powered by two batteries and which magnifies 30 times. It fits into a pocket easily and can be used to look at all sorts of things, from creepy-crawlies to plant cells. Pocket microscopes cost about £5.

They also sell proper microscopes which come complete with a kit of microscope slides and various accessories. These are more expensive (they cost about £40) but they magnify up to 750 times and have a zoom lens. You can also buy these microscopes from the Science Museum. Write to Science Museum Brainwaves, Harrington Dock, Liverpool X, L70 1AX and they will send you a catalogue that also advertises all sorts of other interesting scientific equipment.

You can buy simple hand lenses, which magnify ten times and will allow you to see large plant cells, from camera shops and opticians. You should be able to get a suitable one for £2 or £3.

• Seeds

You will be able to buy most of the seeds you need from your local pet shop or garden centre, but if you cannot find what you need, send for catalogues from:

Suttons Seeds
Hele Road
Torquay
Devon
TQ2 7QJ

Mr Fothergill's Seeds Ltd
Gazeley Road
Kentford
Newmarket
Suffolk
CB8 7QB

Thompson and Morgan
London Road
Ipswich
Suffolk
IP2 0BA

You can get flowerpots and seed compost from garden centres. Several major stores, like Woolworths, stock seeds and garden supplies, but they do not always stock these all the year round. They usually have the widest choice in spring.

• Odds and ends

You can buy bendy straws for potometers from shops like Woolworths, which sell supplies for children's parties, or you can get free ones if you buy small cartons of drink in supermarkets. Some drinks are sold in bags, with narrow plastic straws that you push through the bag. These straws are useful for making the water thermometer in chapter six. You can also get narrow plastic tube from hardware stores.

You can buy thermometers for measuring temperature from chemist shops, from garden centres or from camera shops that sell equipment for developing films.

Most of the other supplies you need, like Clingfilm, kitchen paper and blotting paper can be bought in stationers or supermarkets.

INDEX

ENVIRONMENTALLY YOURS
Early Times

What is the greenhouse effect? Why is the Earth getting warmer? Who is responsible for the destruction of the countryside? Where can you get advice on recycling? When will the Earth's resources run out? The answers to all these questions and many more are given in this forthright and informative book. Topics such as transport, industry, agriculture, population and energy are covered as well as lists of 'green' organizations and useful addresses.

ANIMAL KIND
Early Times

Animal Kind looks at what humans are doing to animals. It also looks at what humans *could* be doing for animals to make their lives happier and to lessen their suffering. This is a hard-hitting book that covers topics such as vivisection, vegetarianism, farming, wildlife, pets and blood sports. It will help you look again at your relationship to the animal world.

DEAR JO
Early Times

Have *you* ever had a real problem like falling out with your best friend; not being able to read properly because of dyslexia; feeling lonely and unloved because your parents have separated; being hooked on *Neighbours* and not able to think of anything else?

Well, maybe you're not alone! Lots of others feel the same way and many of them ask for help by writing to advice columnists like Jo in the *Early Times*. Just telling someone else about your problems can make things better, and getting a helpful, kind and often funny letter back can soon put a smile back on the glummest of faces!

In this book you'll find the answers to lots of problems you may have had, or are likely to have while you're growing up. Some are serious, some more light-hearted – so have a good read, a bit of a giggle and *do* stop worrying!

WAR BOY
Michael Foreman

Barbed wire and barrage balloons, gas masks and Anderson shelters, loud bangs and piercing whines – the sights and sounds of war were all too familiar to a young boy growing up in the 1940s. Lowestoft, a quiet seaside town in Suffolk, was in the front line during World War II. Bombing raids, fires and trips to the air-raid shelters became almost daily events for young Michael Foreman and his friends.

NOAH'S CHOICE
True stories of extinction and survival
David Day

David Day has some shocking stories to tell. Passing fads of fashion have been responsible for the extermination of whole species of birds and animals, and scientists themselves wiped out the last herd of Dwarf Caribou – in an effort to prove to each other that such an animal existed!

But there are also some spectacular survival stories, like that of the Golden Hamster, whose world population rose from thirteen to several million within ten years. Most conservation projects are rather slower to succeed, but here are many heartening descriptions of animals rescued from the brink of extinction.

As we learn from the terrible mistakes of the past, the battle to save our wildlife is on. And its importance has never been greater.

FAME! WHO'S WHO IN HISTORY AT MADAME TUSSAUD'S
Wendy Cooling

Find out about kings, queens, politicians, authors, dictators, idols, plotters and peacemakers. You'll also be able to discover which other famous events happened in the world during the centuries in which they lived.

Some people are only famous for a short time. EVERYONE in this book has earned themselves a lasting place in history and in the most famous hall of fame – Madame Tussaud's.

Non-fiction from Dick King-Smith

COUNTRY WATCH

Animal watching can be fascinating and fun – if you know what to look out for and how best to observe it. There are so many different kinds of animals to see in the British countryside and it's not only the unusual ones that are interesting. *Country Watch* is full of surprising facts (did you know that the tiny mole can burrow its way through thirty pounds of earth in an hour?) and Dick King-Smith has lots of marvellous stories to tell about his own encounters with animals over the years.

TOWN WATCH

It's surprising how many wild animals there are to be seen it towns today. *Town Watch* is crammed with information about the many mammals, birds, insects and reptiles that live within the bounds of our towns and cities. Did you know that the cheeky house-sparrow is really one of the tough guys of the bird world, roaming the city in gangster-style mobs? From rubbish-tip pests like rats and cock-roaches to protected species such as owls and bats, this book has a wealth of information and stories about urban wildlife.

WATER WATCH

If you look at a map of the world, you'll see that most of its surface is sea. We are surrounded by water – all around us there are lakes, ponds, rivers and streams – not to mention man-made waterways like canals. On holiday at the seaside you can enjoy identifying all the different kinds of gull, or if you're near a rocky coastline you might even see a seal! And there are all sorts of water birds – some with very unusual habits – living near lakes and marshes. You'd have to be lucky to spot an otter but if you're patient and observant, there are some fascinating animals to be spotted in and around a garden or village pond.

LAND AHOY! THE STORY OF CHRISTOPHER COLUMBUS
Scoular Anderson

The colour of the sea was probably the last thing that Christopher Columbus was thinking about when he set off, five hundred years ago, on one of the greatest voyages of discovery ever made. His journey was just as adventurous and just as important as the first space flight to the moon was this century. But Columbus set sail into the best ocean not really knowing where he was going or, once he had got there, what he'd found!

Now you can be an explorer by reading this book and finding out just what an extraordinary man Columbus was – how he managed to travel the world and put America on the map for the first time.

PUFFIN BOOK OF ROYAL LONDON
Scoular Anderson

Nowadays the word palace can mean any grand building, but this is a book about a very special group of palaces – the Royal Palaces of London – where the kings and queens of Britain lived and where the present Queen lives today.

Find out which were the favourite palaces and which one had a nasty pong; how the royals got about before cars, trains and buses; why they were sometimes sentenced to death and executed at the Tower; what they did for entertainment and what they ate at the royal banquets! Banquets, beefeaters and beheadings abound in this hilarious guide to Royal London.

WELL, WELL, WELL
Dr Peter Rowan

Find out what your body can (and can't) do; how its many parts work together to keep you healthy; what happens when things go wrong and who and what can make you better. Dr Pete gives some top tips on how to keep yourself fit, as well as some breath-taking facts which will amaze and amuse you.

EUROPE: UP AND AWAY
Sue Finnie

A lively book packed with information about Western Europe which includes sections on stamps, car numbers and languages as well as topics related to an individual country (from Flamenco dancing to frogs' legs).

WATCH OUT: Keeping safe outdoors
Rosie Leyden and Suzanne Ahwai

A book to give children an awareness of the dangers lurking outside on the roads, on their bikes, near water, on building sites, etc. It is full of fun, puzzles and quizzes as well as being packed with information on how to stay safe.

THE ANIMAL QUIZ BOOK
Sally Kilroy

Why do crocodiles swallow stones? Which bird migrates the furthest? Can kangaroos swim? With over a million species, the animal kingdom provides a limitless source of fascinating questions. In this book Sally Kilroy has assembled a feast for enquiring minds — from domestic animals to dinosaurs, fish to footprints, reptiles to record breakers. Discover where creatures live, how they adapt to their conditions, the way they treat each other, the dangers they face — you'll be surprised how much you didn't know.

CAN YOU GET WARTS FROM TOUCHING TOADS?

Dr Peter Rowan

TV-AM's Dr Peter answers questions that children ask him on every subject from warts to hiccups, to the speed at which a sneeze travels.

WORD PUZZLES

David Smith and Veronica Millington

An entertaining collection of puzzles covering a wide variety of areas of interest.

PETS FOR KEEPS

Dick King-Smith

Keeping a pet can be fascinating and great fun. You don't have to be an expert either. But it is important to choose the right pet: one that will fit in with your family and surroundings, one that you can afford to keep, one that you will enjoy looking after, and – most important – one that will be happy with you. This book is packed with useful information about budgies, hamsters, cats, guinea-pigs, mice, rabbits, gerbils, canaries, bantams, rats, goldfish and dogs.